vegetarian
salad for dinner

Sweet Sesame Barley, Kale, Tofu

vegetarian salad for dinner

INVENTIVE PLANT-FORWARD MEALS

jeanne kelley

PHOTOGRAPHY BY THE INGALLS

RIZZOLI
NEW YORK

contents

INTRODUCTION 10 / SALAD GREENS 13 / SALAD PANTRY & TOOL KIT 19

classic salads

Italian Chopped Salad / 24

Warm Brussels Sprout
Caesar, Poached Egg / 27

Korean Bibimbap-Style Salad,
Soy Egg / 29

Potato Salad, Lettuce Cups,
Herb Gribiche / 33

Eggplant Caponata, Ricotta Salata,
Celery Leaves / 34

Chinese "No Chicken" Salad / 37

Indonesian Gado-Gado Salad,
Spicy Peanut Sauce / 38

Salade Provençal, Panisse,
Lemon-Chèvre Dressing / 41

Tostada Salad, Creamy
Lime-Avocado Dressing / 43

Baby Gem, Hearts of Palm,
Avocado, Radish, Marcona
Almonds, Green Goddess / 47

Lettuce Cups, Thai Flavors,
Cauliflower-Tempeh / 48

Vietnamese-Style Salad Rolls,
Hoisin Peanut Sauce / 51

Greek Salad, Greek Fava Dip / 53

grain salads

Carrot, Bulgur, Green Olives,
Arugula, Date, Preserved Lemon / 58

Grape (or Plum), Fennel Tabbouleh,
Goat Cheese "Cream," Saba / 61

Sweet Sesame Barley, Kale, Tofu / 62

Pink Rice, Long Bean, Lime Leaf,
Fresh Turmeric, Sambal Egg / 65

Black Rice, Snap Peas, Pea Sprouts,
Black Garlic Tofu / 67

Crispy Farro, Winter Greens,
Persimmon, Pomegranate,
Hazelnuts / 71

Zucchini and Freekeh Salad,
Za'atar, Halloumi / 72

Summer Succotash Salad,
Herb Dressing / 75

Brussels Sprouts, Wild Rice,
Ancho-Spiced Pecans, Dates,
Goat Cheese / 76

Brown Rice, Grape Leaf Salad / 79

Mushroom, Barley Salad,
Dandelion Greens / 80

Charred Green Beans and Parsnips,
Farro, Radicchio, Gorgonzola,
Walnuts / 83

Arroz con Cosas
(Paella-Style Salad) / 84

contents continued

OPPOSITE PAGE, CLOCKWISE FROM TOP: Arroz con Cosas (Paella-Style Salad); Chopped Salad, Migas, Spanish Goodies; Dandelion Greens, Roasted Potatoes, Romesco

pulse salads

Corona Bean Salad / 88

French Lentils, Roasted Beets, Dried Cherries, Rosemary, Goat Cheese / 91

Muhammara, Turnip, Pomegranate, and Dandelion Green Slaw, Walnuts / 92

Falafel-ette Salad / 95

Beet Hummus, Fioretto, Pine Nut Gremolata / 97

Hummus Msabaha, Curly Endive, Zhoug / 101

Black Lentil, Roast Cauliflower, Red Cabbage Slaw, Piri Piri Sauce / 102

Black Beans, Brown Rice, Scorched Kale / 105

White Bean, Broiled Treviso, Fig, Olive / 106

Potato, Pea, Mango, Yogurt, Spice, Spinach / 109

Grilled Broccoli, Mushrooms, Peppers, White Bean Purée, Chimichurri / 110

Mung Beans, Caramelized Onions, Sun-Dried Tomatoes / 113

salads with seeds

Quinoa, Spring Vegetables, Arugula, Kumquats, Pistachios / 116

Roasted Spiced Carrots, Quinoa, Chickpeas, Green Ribbons, Turmeric Vinaigrette / 119

Acorn Squash, Wilted Red Cabbage, Apple, Pumpkin Seed Dressing / 121

Grilled Sweet Potatoes, Kale, Garlicky Yogurt, Puffed Buckwheat / 125

Red Quinoa and Red Kidney Bean Masala / 126

Coconut Quinoa, Black Beans, Avocado, Mango, Collards, Plantain, Cashews / 129

Black Quinoa, Black Lentils, Pomegranate, Orange, Honey Baked Feta / 130

Beet, Buckwheat, Walnuts, Greens, Goat Gouda / 133

Kohlrabi, Avocado, Egg, Radicchio, Watercress, Mustard-Poppy Vinaigrette / 134

Heirloom Salad, Creamy Sesame-Miso Tofu / 137

Spa Salad with Seeds, Free-Free Dressing / 138

pasta salads

Pesto Zoodles and Noodles / 142

Buckwheat Soba, Kabocha Squash, Walnuts, Persimmon, Greens / 145

Saffron Gem Couscous, Smashed Cucumbers with Mint, Greens, Pomegranate Vinaigrette / 147

Fregola, Fennel, Olive, Pecorino, Orange, Arugula / 151

Artichoke with Sambuca, Pasta, Ricotta Salata / 152

Fava Beans, Asparagus, Toasted Couscous, Spring Herbs, Preserved Lemon, Labneh / 155

Orecchiette, Tomato-Herb Salsa Cruda / 156

Roasted Broccoli, Preserved Lemon, Calabrian Chile, Whole Wheat Pasta / 158

Loaded Orzo / 159

Ginger-Sesame Noodles, Salad, Cashews / 160

bread salads

Egg Salad, Ricotta, Herbs,
Sprouted Grain Toasties / 164

Arugula Cacio e Pepe Pizza / 167

Breaded Baked Goat Cheese, Frisée,
Wild Mushrooms, Asparagus / 169

Herby Fattoush, Sumac-Cumin
Pita Crisps / 173

Chopped Salad, Migas, Spanish
Goodies / 175

Broccoli Salad with Olive,
Pecorino, Lemon, Croutons / 179

Summer Panzanella, Burrata,
Pesto Drizzle / 180

Fall Bread Salad / 183

Spring Panzanella,
Creamy Pecorino Dressing / 184

roasted & toasted salads

Chickpeas, Cauliflower, Tomato,
Sumac Yogurt / 188

Whole Roasted Cauliflower, Mung
Beans, Greens, Black Tahini / 191

Salade "Gratinée," Roasted Fingerlings,
Red Onions / 192

Dandelion Greens, Roasted Potatoes,
Romesco / 195

Roasted Whole Butternut Squash,
Salsa Macha, Kale,
Cotija Cheese / 196

Roasted Delicata, Goat Cheese,
Arugula, Almond Charmoul / 199

Roasted Asparagus, Broccolini,
Feta, Meyer Lemon, Green Garlic,
Arugula, Pistachio Dukkah / 200

Tempeh, Spinach, Peanutty-Lime
Dressing / 203

Roasted Beets, Citrus, Labneh,
Zhoug / 204

Baked Ricotta Pepperonata,
Herb Salad / 207

North African–Style Chickpea
Pancake, Salad Turnips, Greens,
Harissa / 208

toppings, sauces, spreads

Harissa / 213

Piri Piri Sauce / 213

Zhoug / 214

Cashew Cream / 214

Salsa Macha / 215

Tamarind Chutney Sauce / 215

Garlicky Yogurt / 215

Pesto Drizzle / 216

Romesco Sauce / 216

Spicy Coconut Peanut Sauce / 218

Preserved Lemons / 218

Ancho-Spiced Pecans / 219

Rustic Croutons / 219

ACKNOWLEDGEMENTS 220 / INDEX 221

PAGES 8-9, CLOCKWISE FROM TOP LEFT CORNER: Herby Fattoush, Sumac-Cumin Pita Crisps (page 173), Chickpeas, Cauliflower, Tomato, Sumac Yogurt (page 188), Muhammara, Turnip, Pomegranate, and Dandelion Green Slaw, Walnuts (page 92), Carrot, Bulgur, Green Olives, Arugula, Date, Preserved Lemon (page 58)

introduction

Here's a book that I hope will fulfill two of your desires: more recipes for original, satisfying salads and more vegetarian dinner solutions. People *love* a good salad. I know because I receive emails from salad fans thanking me for the recipes in my previous salad book, *Salad for Dinner*. I also understand the effort that goes into vegetarian meal planning and the need for nourishing and balanced plant-forward meals. The salads in this collection aim to become part of your dinner rotation whether you know your way around a kitchen and garden or not.

These salads have flavors and ingredients influenced by the many culinary heritages in my hometown of Los Angeles and by my travels. They are also inspired by the abundant produce of my garden and farmers' markets, and from occasional glances at cookbooks and blogs. As a cook who has tried to re-create and adapt delicious dishes from kitchens around the world to satisfy my cravings, I hope that these efforts are viewed as tribute rather than appropriation.

My interpretation of "salad" is loosely tossed. There are recipes for traditional tossed and chopped salads, there are recipes for classic cooked salads in the Italian tradition, but there are also salads that eat like a deconstructed sandwich and salads that resemble grain bowls, mezze, and pasta dishes. There's even a recipe for a salad-topped "cacio e pepe" pizza. To anyone who might balk at my inclusivity, I assure you that you will welcome the variety of tasty dinners—and that I shared my cherished and perfected recipe for pizza dough.

While there is so much in this book that will inspire those who have spent a lifetime eschewing meat, I would like to note that I am not a strict vegetarian. I am a cook and vegetable lover who enjoys a plant-forward diet. I grew up in a meat-eating, hunting, and fishing home. When I travel, I taste the local specialty, even if it's meaty. If I am invited over for your grandma's Bolognese, I'll bring a nice bottle of wine to enjoy with it, and as a native Angeleno, I indulge in occasional visits to the taco truck or taqueria. I note this because I believe that my being flexitarian helps me create recipes that are satisfying to vegetarians and omnivores alike.

I also make liberal use of cheese and yogurt in my salads, but I include a simple recipe for a dairy-free cheese for people looking to reduce or eliminate dairy in their diet. And with so many good vegan cheese and yogurt options, the recipes can be easily adapted. Eggs star in some of the salads too, as they are an excellent source of protein, and because a flock of happy hens is part of my garden's ecosystem.

The book is divided into categories where a standard or element is shared: Classic, Grain, Pulse, Seeds, Pasta, Bread, and Roasted and Toasted. There's an overlap of ingredients and techniques in the sections, but the book is organized in a way that's meant to help with meal planning. The salads feature an array of vegetables, handy when your garden or CSA box yields a variety or an abundance of produce. There are also a few recipes that have been featured in previous books of mine that I have updated to reflect my ever-evolving style of cooking and resources.

Many of the salads are hearty, one-dish dinners, but others are light—the kind of refreshment that one might want to eat to cap off a day of heavy lunching or to enjoy as an appetizer. Mostly, each dish is crafted to be a main event. For people concerned about a possible lack of protein from a vegetarian diet, there's recent medical sentiment that we should all eat more plants and worry less about protein consumption. Because most of the foods we eat from morning until night contain small amounts of protein, the tally of grams by day's end generally meets our RDA. Here you'll find the salad to fit your desires— whether it be a super-health-conscious chopped salad to kick-start a wellness plan, an indulgent tossed salad, or a party-perfect platter salad, the right recipe is here.

salad greens

Not every salad in this book features salad greens, but a good portion do—after all, cool, crisp lettuce leaves are what most salads are all about. There are two schools of thought when it comes to salad greens. There is the slightly old-fashioned sense that the greens should be a neutral vehicle for salad dressings and goodies, and then there are people like me who appreciate and want to celebrate the freshness and flavor of the greens themselves. I like to spike my salad bowl with the wasabi-like punch of red mustard leaves, but I also appreciate the appropriate place for a tender, sweet leaf of folded Bibb. "Salad greens" can refer to any number of leafy vegetables used in salad; mixtures can include not only lettuces, but spinach, kale, mustards, tender young chard, beet and pea leaves, and leafy herbs such as arugula, sorrel, and flat-leaf Italian parsley.

A GLOSSARY OF SALAD GREENS

Arugula: If I could pick only one favorite salad green, it would have to be arugula. I love its bold, peppery flavor and the way it stands up to strong meats, cheeses, and sauces but does not overwhelm more delicately flavored vegetables, eggs, and pasta. There are several varieties of arugula, from giant, twelve-inch leaf varieties to tiny wild arugula with its pretty, deeply serrated leaves. Sometimes called rocket or roquette, arugula is technically a spring green, but it goes so well with robust summery flavors, especially those of the Mediterranean where it originated, that, luckily for us, it's available in markets year-round.

Baby Beet, Pea, and Fava Bean Leaves: Baby beet, pea, and fava bean leaves all make attractive and interesting additions to salads, but unless you garden, some of these greens might be hard to come by. If you purchase bunches of baby beets, there are often very small leaves at the center of the beet top. Clip, wash, and add these red-veined leaves to your salad mix. Pea tendrils are gaining in popularity and show up in the spring at farmers' markets and specialty food stores and are available year-round at Chinese markets. I prefer using the pea-flavored leaves and discarding the wiry tendril. Fava leaves have a slight artichoke flavor; the plant grows like a weed, so consider planting a bean or two, if only for the leaves.

Belgian Endive: Belgian endive forms small, slender oval heads that are white with a touch of either chartreuse or burgundy at the leaf tip. This member of the common chicory family is forced, meaning that it does the majority of its growing under sand to keep the heads from turning green (or red) and leafing out. The narrow, spoon-like spears are best used as whole separated leaves, cut lengthwise into strips, or cut crosswise into rounds.

OPPOSITE: Spring Panzanella, Creamy Pecorino Dressing, page 184

Butter Lettuce and Salanova: Butterhead, Bibb, Boston, and Limestone are names for this delicate, mild-flavored lettuce. The tight, ruffled heads have velvety soft leaves and tender, butter-yellow folds in the center. There are countless varieties of butterhead lettuces to plant or source at farmers' markets, including red-tinged heirlooms such as Sierra. Butter lettuces are heat-resistant and grow in the spring, summer, and fall. At the market, look for firm heads for the best value. Salanova is a type of Bibb lettuce that was developed in the Netherlands. The lettuce grows in lush rosette-like heads that are bolt-resistant. Varieties include red-, green-, oak-, and round-leaf heads. It's derived from a baby lettuce that's allowed to mature, thus becoming more flavorful. Salanova is very easy to grow, and I usually have several heads growing in my garden from fall to spring.

Cabbage: Cabbage adds body and crunch to salads and slaws. If you use red cabbage, then you've got deep purple to add to your color palette. Cabbage is mild and sweet but should be sliced very thinly, as the leaves are tough. French savoy cabbage with its crinkly leaves offers up a variety of textures in a slaw while napa cabbage, or Chinese cabbage, features a large, tender, white spine. Bok choy is another variety of Chinese cabbage, and baby bok choy makes a nice, sturdy salad green.

Collard Greens: Collard greens are another member of the brassica family. Popular worldwide and commonly associated with Southern cuisine, collards are like kale nutritionally. The leaves grow quite large, about the size of a fourteen-inch oval platter, making them perfect to cut into long ribbons for salads or to use blanched or raw in place of grain-based wraps.

Curly Endive: Curly endive is a chicory like Belgian endive. Bitter, with pale and dark green and very curly leaves, it is sometimes confused with frisée. Curly endive is larger, darker, and wider, with a more pronounced bitter flavor than frisée. Curly endive is more common than frisée and is available at most markets. Use it to add depth to chopped salad mixes. It's also very good cooked.

Dandelion Greens: As a kid, when I pondered the blossom of a dandelion, I figured the name was English, a mash-up of "dandy" and "lion," as the flowers looked like a snappy cartoon version of the king of cats. But the name is derived from the French *dents de lion*, or "lion's teeth," because of the jagged teeth appearance of the leaves. When I lived in the southwest of France, I learned another name for the weed that we would forage for in the countryside. *Le pis-en-lit*, so named because of the greens' diuretic qualities, is popular served with a warm vinaigrette. Despite enjoying the salad, I luckily did not wet the bed. Foraged dandelion greens, when picked very small, add a pleasant bitterness to a peppery greens mix. Cultivated dandelion greens range from mild to very bitter and should be tasted before using.

Escarole: Escarole is a mildly bitter chicory with broad, sturdy leaves that grow in flat rosettes. My husband started growing it for me a few years ago and it has become a new favorite of the bitter greens. The large heads last a long time in the refrigerator or garden, so it's a good "storing" green. Escarole stands up to strongly flavored dressings and is tasty wilted or cooked.

Frisée: Frisée adds great flavor, texture, and color to salad mixes, but it is also wonderful when served on its own. Often marketed as "baby frisée" so as not to be confused with curly endive, it lacks endive's bitterness. Frisée has narrow leaves with frilly ends and grows in green and harder-to-find red varieties. When I don't have frisée growing in my garden, I find it at the farmers' market.

Green and Red Salad Bowl Lettuce: These are the large, ruffled heads available at the supermarket. Sometimes simply labeled "red-leaf" or "green-leaf" lettuce, this is the most popular of the loose-leaf variety of lettuce. Loose-leaf lettuces grow in a rosette shape. Great varieties to grow or search out at the farmers' market include Lollo Rosso, Cocarde, and Deer Tongue.

Herbs: Mild, leafy herbs such as basil, chervil, cilantro, dill, Italian (flat-leaf) parsley, and sorrel make bold additions to salad blends. Herbs are best used in salad mixes where they won't compete with or overshadow the other ingredients in the salad. Salads that feature strong cheeses are great with herbs in the mix.

Kale: Kale is a popular green that is related to cabbage. There are many great varieties, including Russian, curly, red, flowering, and lacinato (aka dinosaur kale, Tuscan kale, or cavolo nero). Kale is usually eaten sautéed or stewed in soups or pastas, but an added acid, such as lemon juice or vinegar, "cooks" kale the way vinaigrette can wilt a salad when it sits too long, resulting in a hearty and virtuous salad. Kale is robust enough that it can also be grilled.

Little Gem Lettuce: Salads made from *Lactuca sativa* have been popping up on the trendiest menus in the past few years. This flavorful lettuce forms small, five- to six-inch heads with lightly ruffled, elongated leaves that in texture resemble a cross between romaine and butter lettuce. This cool-season lettuce tastes nutty and so sweet that the French name for it is *sucrine,* from the word *sucre,* meaning "sugar."

Mâche: Mâche is a small, delicate salad green. With their vibrant grass-green color and subtle, nutty flavor, the tongue-shaped leaves and small rosettes make a pretty addition to baby salad mixes. Also called lamb's lettuce or corn salad, mâche is available at specialty foods stores.

Mizuna: Mizuna is a Japanese mustard with feathery leaves and a spicy flavor. Mizuna is often used in stir-fries but tastes great raw, either on its own or as part of a peppery mix of greens. Mizuna is often included in purchased salad blends but can be hard to find on its own. Look for it at Japanese markets or consider growing some.

Oakleaf Lettuce: Oakleaf lettuce is an heirloom loose-leaf variety. Oakleaf grows in red, green, and speckled rosette-shaped heads. The small heads feature a wide, crunchy center spine and tender lobes that are similar in shape to the leaves of a white oak tree.

Puntarelle: Puntarelle is a rare Roman chicory. In Italian, *puntarelle* translates as "little tips," a good description for the outer leaves on the head of the chicory. The interior heart is thinly sliced and soaked in water, which lessens the bitterness and causes the shreds to curl. Prized for its bittersweet flavor, puntarelle is available in the late fall and early winter. I don't call for the exotic green in any of the following recipes (it's too hard to find), but if you luck out and find yourself with some, both the leaves and the stalks would be wonderful celebrated in Italian Chopped Salad (page 24) or garnishing the Baked Ricotta Pepperonata (page 207). For a side salad, toss it with the Warm Brussels Sprouts Caesar Dressing (page 27).

Purslane: Purslane is a salad herb with thick teardrop-shaped leaves and a citrusy, tart, and succulent taste. It's high in omega-3 fatty acids and grows as a crop, ground cover (portulaca), and weed. While it is sometimes available at Middle Eastern markets, you'll have better chances sourcing it at Mexican markets, where it is called *verdolaga*. Purslane is also available at farmers' markets in the summer months.

Radicchio and Treviso: Radicchio is another member of the chicory family. For the radicchio to form a tight dark purple head with the characteristic white veins, it must be either blanched (a process of bundling and tying the outer leaves of the plant around the center) on the winter field or aged in a dark, wet shed. Regardless of how it is cultivated, this colorful and deliciously bitter salad green is available at most markets year-round. A close relative of radicchio is Treviso. Treviso forms an elongated head with wide, white, edible spines. It's slightly less bitter than radicchio and also benefits from year-round availability.

Red Mustard: Bronze-leafed red mustard is another favorite of mine. I love the color that the leaves add to salads as well as the strong Dijon-mustard-meets-wasabi flavor. The large, tender leaves are good cooked, wilted, and, in small doses, raw. I grow red mustard by the bundle, but it's often available at farmers' markets and specialty foods stores. If you plan to eat the mustard raw, look for perky leaves that are not wilted.

Romaine: Romaine or cos lettuce has a characteristic thick spine and elongated leaves. This is a hardy lettuce that grows well in cool to cold weather. Romaine lettuce heads can get as large as fifteen inches tall and come in green and red varieties. Rosalita, with red speckles, and Rouge d'Hiver, with burgundy leaves, are particularly pretty types. When I want crunch in a salad, I use romaine—often chopped or sliced.

Spinach: Freshly picked spinach is a springtime treat, but almost as tasty and extra convenient are the readily available packages of prewashed organic spinach. Small spinach leaves stand up to the "triple washing," packaging, and shipping better than tender lettuces do. Baby spinach is great on its own or tossed into the salad mix. Mature spinach, however, will often get chalky in taste and squeak against the teeth, so it's best cooked.

Swiss Chard: Chard is a member of the beet family cultivated for its leaves instead of its root. Chard is generally cooked, but tiny baby leaves can be added to salad mixes and larger, still-tender leaves can be thinly sliced off the stalk and added to salad. Usually what's on offer at the grocery store is too mature or too wilted for eating raw, so look for chard at the farmers' market. Chard is an excellent vegetable to plant. Available in so many colorful varieties (there's one called rainbow), it can grow year-round and even in the snow.

Tatsoi: Tatsoi, like mizuna, is another popular Asian salad green. The leaves are spoon-shaped, hence it's sometimes called spoon cabbage. When small, tatsoi is sold as loose, two- to three-inch leaves. But it actually grows in a rosette, similar to baby bok choy, and will sometimes be sold that way. It has a mild mustard-meets-cabbage flavor.

Watercress: Cress is simply a leafy vegetable, and watercress is cress that grows in water. Some markets sell bunches of cut watercress and others vend a live, hydroponically grown type with a roots-in-foam appendage. The hydroponic variety is very mild. Watercress can also be foraged from clean brooks and ponds, and I highly recommend it—it's fresh, peppery, and free.

OPPOSITE: Quinoa, Spring Vegetables, Arugula, Kumquats, Pistachios, page 116

salad pantry & tool kit

Making satisfying meals is relatively easy in a well-stocked kitchen. It's like playing cards with a full deck. Stocking the salad pantry isn't all that different from stocking a basic kitchen pantry, but a plant-forward pantry needs more flavor boosters. In theory, our cupboards should contain everything we need to cook meals for a week or weeks, with weekly or biweekly trips to the farmers' market or greengrocer for fresh produce. It doesn't always work this way, but it sure tastes good when it does.

All kitchens should house basic bulk pantry items such as pasta, assorted grains, seeds from quinoa to pumpkin, nuts, and dried pulses (beans and lentils). Cupboards should hold canned and jarred goods like beans, coconut milk, tahini, peanut butter, and honey. A vegetarian pantry benefits from a little more thought and planning. Specialty items specific to a salad are described in the individual recipes, but here's a general guideline for a well-stocked salad pantry.

PANTRY

Oil: I keep the selection of oils in my pantry and refrigerator streamlined. Because flavor is foremost to me, I choose not to cook with vegetable oil, canola oil, and the like. I might fry tortilla strips in organic corn oil if I have it on hand, but I don't stock it regularly.

Olive oil: I use extra-virgin olive for all recipes calling for olive oil. It's standard culinary practice that extra-virgin olive oil isn't used for cooked dishes because it has a low smoke point (the temperature at which it burns) and because heating the oil destroys the flavor. Many cooks keep less expensive "regular" olive oil for cooking and extra virgin for uncooked foods. I use a lot of olive oil, and if I were to do a cost-benefit analysis, I'd find that stocking and storing regular olive oil isn't worth the thought and space and extra-virgin olive oil makes for really delicious fried panisse, sautéed Brussels sprouts, and roasted potatoes. An exception to my one-bottle rule is made for

extra-fancy virgin olive oil, usually a gift or souvenir, that I will drizzle to add a finishing dazzle.

Nut oils: Hazelnut oil and walnut oil are robust oils that add a warm, nutty flavor to salads. I store them in the refrigerator so they won't go rancid between uses. Peanut oil is a versatile oil. It's my go-to for frying (it has a very high smoke point) and is good in dressings. Most peanut oil is mild, but toasted and roasted peanut oils have a rich, peanutty taste.

Seed oils: Sesame oil, like peanut oil, comes in toasted and untoasted versions. Toasted sesame oil, often called Asian or dark sesame oil, has a strong sesame flavor. I make dressing with untoasted sesame oil, as it's very light. I use the toasted variety in dishes with an Asian influence. Pumpkin seed oil is very dark and rich. It's used as a finishing oil.

Vinegar: I've allotted a good amount of cupboard space to vinegar. Vinegar is great for adding acid and flavor to all food, not just salad. A splash of fancy Banyuls (a barrel-aged vinegar made from sweet wine in the South of France) or balsamic vinegar can transform roasted grapes from interesting to exciting. There are many good-tasting specialty vinegars being made, with flavors from pear to pomegranate to honey. For consistency in this book I focus primarily on the standards: apple cider vinegar, balsamic vinegar, Chinese black vinegar, Champagne vinegar, red wine vinegar, rice vinegar (not seasoned), sherry vinegar, and white wine vinegar. It's important to note that all vinegars vary widely in acidity. One brand of red wine vinegar might be milder and sweeter than the next, so be sure to always taste and adjust dressings and vinaigrettes before using. As standard as most of these vinegars are, they are getting increasingly hard to find. Chain markets both basic and specialty devote so much space to balsamic vinegar that staples such as white wine and sherry vinegar have been squeezed off the shelf. Italian markets and French specialty stores are great places to get large bottles of good-quality wine vinegars at affordable prices. For Chinese black vinegar, you might have to resort to online shopping, but a good substitution is provided. Also note that Chinese black vinegar typically is not gluten-free, so do use the noted substitution in any recipe that is tagged as "GF option."

Condiments: Good condiments have always been food's playground, but they are especially important to plant-forward cooking. Fermented condiments like Calabrian chiles and miso paste are great for adding umami to vegetarian dishes.

Stock basics like Dijon mustard and mayonnaise. Look to the "Asian" section of the market for soy sauce (I especially like Japanese tamari, and most versions of tamari are gluten-free), gochujang, hoisin, sambal oelek, sriracha sauce, kimchi, miso paste (I like mellow white miso), and fish sauce, either the delicious Red Boat brand for "flexitarians" like myself or a vegan variety.

Olives, Pickles, and Preserves: Stock a variety of green and black olives. The green ones should be Cerignola or Castelvetrano, picholine or Lucques, and for the black, kalamata, Niçoise, and pungent oil-cured ones should be on hand. Next to your olives you should store capers, cornichons (gherkins), sun-dried tomatoes, crunchy Italian lupini beans, and homemade or purchased preserved lemons.

Spice Rack: Your spice rack should keep the heavy hitters like black pepper, paprika, dried oregano, and red pepper flakes. Other readily available spices to have on hand include ancho chile powder, coriander seeds, cumin (whole and ground), fennel seeds, whole cardamom pods, saffron, smoked paprika, and turmeric. If you like spicy foods, keep arbol, chipotle, and guajillo chiles in a dry place. You'll have to make a special trip to a Middle Eastern market or find an online source for Aleppo pepper, ground sumac, and za'atar, but the reward in terms of punchy flavor is worth the effort. Spice purveyors such as Penzeys and Diaspora Co. offer excellent-quality products, with the latter focusing on direct-from-the-farmer spices.

Dairy and Nondairy Substitutes: Yogurt, Greek yogurt, labneh, and sour cream are salad basics. When suitable, I offer the option of using Greek yogurt, labneh, and sour cream interchangeably. For recipes that really benefit from the mild cheese flavor of labneh or need that characteristic tang from yogurt or the sweet sourness of sour cream, I call those ingredients out specifically. When I call out plain yogurt, I'm referring to pourable Euro-style yogurt. I always purchase full-fat yogurt because I prefer the flavor and texture. For people who eschew dairy, there are several nondairy yogurts at the market—just be sure to choose a plain vegan yogurt with no added sugars. Culina brand makes a very good Greek-style vegan yogurt.

The cheese drawer should house good keepers like Parmesan and feta, but otherwise you might have to make a trip to the cheese shop. For vegans, there are many vegan cheeses available for purchase, or try my simple Cashew Cream (page 214).

Crunchy Additions: A sprinkle of something crunchy is a great way to finish a salad. Crispy onions, plantain chips, crunchy spiced chickpea snacks, spicy Indian snack mix, seasoned Japanese rice crackers, Parmesan crisps, spiced nuts, and tortilla chips are great for adding pop to salads. Making a batch of crispy croutons on the weekend to store in an airtight tin for use throughout the week is another great crunch hack.

Salt: I use fine sea salt for cooking and baking, flaked sea salt such as Maldon or Jacobsen flakes for finishing, and kosher salt for preserving citrus.

TOOL KIT

I try to keep my kitchen equipment to a minimum, but as these salads are main courses, they require a little more preparation. Besides the kitchen basics of good knives, cutting boards, mixing bowls, saucepans, skillets, and measuring cups and spoons, there are a few other kitchen tools necessary for outfitting a well-equipped salad station.

A quality **salad spinner** is a must if you want to avoid soggy salads and watered-down dressings. I've been making salads long enough that I remember trying to dry salad greens by layering them between paper towels or swinging the leaves in a small hammock fashioned from a dish towel—neither very effective methods. Washing, drying, and storing greens is easy and efficient with a spinner.

A large, wide, **4- to 8-cup measuring cup** allows you to measure lettuce without crushing it and takes away the guesswork.

A **blender** and **food processor** make speedy work of blended dressings, sauces and purees. A Nutribullet is particularly handy for whipping up small amounts of dressing.

Another excellent time-saver is a **julienne peeler**. With a few quick strokes, carrots, cucumbers, and large radishes are cut into perfect thin julienne strips. You can find this nifty tool at kitchen shops.

My favorite kitchen tools include a **Japanese ginger grater** (great for garlic too), a **Microplane grater** for extra-fine zest, and **hinged citrus juicers** because they are fast and extract flavorful oils from the skin when juicing. Included in this list is an inexpensive handheld **mini mandoline** or **V-slicer** for cutting extra-thin vegetable slices that are both so pretty and nice to eat.

Lastly, **large wide salad bowls** and **salad servers** for gently mixing and tossing, and for serving up a fresh and pretty creation.

classic salads

These salads, while not exactly standards, are united by a classic theme. Some are meatless takes on favorites such as the Italian Chopped Salad and the Chinese "No Chicken" Salad, while others like the Caponata, Gado-Gado, and Vietnamese-Style Spring Rolls stay true to their roots. But I also include recipes that are riffs on well-known dishes, like a salad version of the Korean rice bowl bibimbap and Thai-inspired salad cups filled with a tempeh and cauliflower stir-fry. A medley of Provençal veggies combined with the chickpea fritters so popular in the region or a potato salad topped with an old-school French egg-and-caper sauce are classic only in the sense that they include ingredients or elements true to a certain region or condiment. These are the pages to turn to for a plant-forward tostada salad, Caesar, or Green Goddess.

italian chopped salad

4 SERVINGS / GF

This colorful and bursting-with-flavor salad will easily sway fans of the classic salami, cheese, and head-lettuce mix served at your local red-sauce spot. Lots of satisfying crunch comes from cabbage and fennel, while the chopped lemon, inspired by a memorable sandwich eaten in Sicily, adds unexpected zest. The taste and texture combo of salty, chewy lupini beans and fiery, fermented Calabrian chiles will trick your brain into thinking that you're munching on Calabrese salami. Look for jars of lupini beans and Calabrian chiles at well-stocked Italian delis or purchase them online.

1 (14- to 16-ounce) can chickpeas, rinsed and drained

4 cups chopped romaine lettuce (about 1 heart)

1 large fennel bulb, trimmed and chopped (about 2 cups)

2 cups chopped red cabbage (about ¼ medium head)

1 yellow bell pepper, chopped

1 small hothouse or 2 Persian or pickling cucumbers, diced

1½ cups halved cherry tomatoes or diced heirloom tomatoes

⅔ cup chopped pitted Italian green olives, such as Cerignola or Castelvetrano

½ cup chopped red onion

½ cup ready-to-eat lupini beans, peeled and rinsed

½ cup chopped fresh Italian parsley leaves

¼ cup chopped fresh basil

1 small lemon

½ cup extra-virgin olive oil

2 tablespoons red wine vinegar

4 jarred Calabrian chiles, stemmed and minced (about 1 generous tablespoon)

2 garlic cloves, finely grated or pressed with a garlic press

½ cup coarsely grated Parmesan cheese

½ cup coarsely grated Fontina, mozzarella, or other mild white cheese

Freshly cracked black pepper

1 tablespoon fresh oregano leaves (optional)

Combine the chickpeas, lettuce, fennel, cabbage, bell pepper, cucumber, tomatoes, olives, onions, beans, parsley, and basil in a large bowl. Trim the ends from the lemon and discard. Cut the lemon in half lengthwise. Thinly slice the lemon and remove the seeds. Chop the lemon slices into small pieces, being careful not to lose the juice. Add the lemon pieces to the bowl. (The salad can be prepared up to 6 hours ahead. Cover and refrigerate.)

Whisk together the oil, vinegar, chiles, and garlic in a small bowl for the dressing. Add the dressing and cheeses to the salad, season generously with black pepper, and toss well. Divide the salad among dishes. Garnish with the oregano, if desired, and serve.

warm brussels sprout caesar, poached egg

2 SERVINGS

A vegetarian variation of the classic salad dressing gets tossed with thinly sliced and lightly sautéed Brussels sprouts in this wonderful fall salad inspired by Los Angeles chef Josef Centeno. Instead of adding the traditional coddled egg to the dressing, the salad is topped with a perfectly poached egg. Enjoy the salad with a glass of chilled chenin blanc—the hints of apple and pear will pair nicely with the funky Brussels sprouts and the wine's high acidity will balance the richness of the egg and Parmesan.

Dressing

¼ cup extra-virgin olive oil

2 tablespoons fresh lemon juice

1 large garlic clove, peeled

1 slightly rounded teaspoon Dijon mustard

1 teaspoon soy sauce or tamari

½ teaspoon lemon zest

1 tablespoon capers

Salt and freshly ground black pepper

Salad

1 pound Brussels sprouts

2 eggs

1 tablespoon white wine vinegar

1 tablespoon extra-virgin olive oil

2 ounces Parmesan cheese, coarsely grated or shaved (about ½ cup)

Freshly cracked black pepper

Parmesan Crostini (recipe follows)

For the dressing: Combine the oil, lemon juice, garlic, mustard, soy sauce or tamari, and lemon zest in a blender and blend until the garlic is finely minced. Add the capers and pulse until the capers are chopped. Season the dressing with salt and pepper. *(The dressing can be prepared up to 2 days ahead; cover and refrigerate.)*

For the salad: Trim the Brussels sprouts and cut them in half from the top to the stem end. Cut the halved sprouts crosswise into thin slices. *(The Brussels sprouts can be prepared up to 2 days ahead; cover and refrigerate.)*

Bring a medium skillet of water to a gentle simmer over medium heat. Add the vinegar to the water. Working with one egg at a time, crack an egg into a small bowl and gently slide the egg into the simmering water in the skillet. Cook, gently pushing simmering water over the tops of the eggs, until the whites are cooked through but the yolks are not set, about 3 minutes. Using a slotted spoon, carefully transfer the eggs to a plate; keep warm.

Heat the oil in a heavy large skillet over medium-high heat. Add the Brussels sprouts and cook until just heated through and beginning to wilt, about 4 minutes. Remove from the heat, add dressing to taste, and toss well. Divide the salad between two shallow bowls and sprinkle with the cheese. Top with the eggs and season with pepper. Serve with Parmesan crostini.

recipe continues

Tip: Don't let egg poaching intimidate you—it's easy. Make sure the poaching liquid (water and vinegar, in this case) is gently simmering with only a soft bubble and a whisper of steam. Cracking the eggs, one at a time, into a small bowl with gently sloped sides helps keep the egg compact and intact when slipping it into the water. Eggs can be poached hours ahead. Simply transfer the eggs from the poaching liquid into a bowl filled with ice water and keep in the refrigerator. The ice water ensures that the eggs will not overcook. When ready to use, reheat by slipping them into simmering water for 30 seconds to 1 minute to warm through.

parmesan crostini

MAKES 12

These crunchy little toasts are not only fun to munch with the Brussels Sprouts Caesar, but with any number of salads in this book including the Italian Chopped (page 24), the White Bean, Broiled Treviso, Fig and Olive (page 106), and most of the pasta salads too. The crostini can also be served as a cocktail nibble or snack, and you can't beat them for dipping into a warm bowl of tomato soup. Using ciabatta or a rustic loaf with large bread holes creates a lacy effect, but the crostini are also good made with long, diagonally cut slices of baguette. You can use pecorino in place of the Parmesan—the toasts will be a little saltier, but a hefty sprinkling of coarse black pepper will cut through that saltiness beautifully.

12 thin slices ciabatta or rustic white bread

Extra-virgin olive oil for brushing

¼ cup freshly grated Parmesan cheese

Freshly cracked black pepper

Preheat the oven to 400°F.

Arrange the bread pieces on a sheet pan and brush with oil. Sprinkle with the cheese and season with pepper. Bake until the crostini are golden brown and toasted, about 10 minutes. *(The crostini can be prepared up to 3 days ahead. Cool and store in an airtight container or resealable plastic bag.)*

korean bibimbap-style salad, soy egg

4 SERVINGS / GF OPTION

Bibimbap is a warming comfort dish of rice, cooked and pickled vegetables, and kimchi, topped with a raw or fried egg. I've translated the traditional Korean dish into a salad, replacing the gooey raw or fried egg with a cold-salad-friendly marinated jammy egg. Just like the original dish, it hits all the bases—spicy, cool, umami, tender, crunchy. The salad also adapts well to what you have on hand and your personal taste. Leftover broccoli? Add it. Don't like kimchi? Omit it. Prefer white rice? Use it. Korean barbecue has become so popular that the fermented chile paste gochujang is available at many supermarkets, but if you can't find it, go ahead and try my cheater mix of miso and sriracha.

Dressing

⅓ cup gochujang, or 2 tablespoons white miso paste mixed with 3 tablespoons sriracha

¼ cup peanut oil or untoasted (light) sesame oil

3 tablespoons Chinese black vinegar or apple cider vinegar

2 tablespoons toasted sesame oil

2 tablespoons honey

2 tablespoons water

2 small garlic cloves, grated or pressed with a garlic press

3 tablespoons toasted sesame seeds

Salad

2 medium carrots, cut into julienne strips

1 (4-inch-long) Korean radish or piece of daikon radish, cut into julienne strips (about 1 cup)

1 Korean, Japanese, or small hothouse cucumber, sliced

¼ cup rice vinegar

Generous pinch of sugar

Salt

2 tablespoons peanut oil or untoasted (light) sesame oil

8 ounces shiitake mushrooms, stemmed and sliced (about 4 cups)

1 tablespoon toasted sesame oil, plus more for drizzling

1 (12-ounce) package bean sprouts (mung or soy; about 5 cups)

1 tablespoon soy sauce or tamari

8 cups mixed bite-sized pieces mixed greens, such as red lettuce, red mustard, baby bok choy, chrysanthemum leaves, and spinach

4 cups cooked brown rice, cooled

4 Soy Eggs (recipe follows)

Kimchi, for garnish

3 green onions, thinly sliced

Toasted sesame seeds, for sprinkling

For the dressing: Whisk together all the ingredients to blend in a small bowl or jar.
(The dressing can be made up to 1 week ahead. Cover and refrigerate.)

recipe continues

For the salad: Combine the carrots, radish, and cucumber in a medium bowl, then add the vinegar and sugar and toss. Sprinkle with salt and toss with your hands, pressing gently with your fingertips to soften the vegetables slightly. Set the mixture aside while you continue with the salad.

Heat the peanut oil in a heavy large skillet over medium-high heat. Add the mushrooms and sauté until they release some moisture, about 3 minutes. Add the toasted sesame oil and bean sprouts and sauté until the mushrooms are tender and the bean sprouts wilt, about 5 minutes longer. Stir in the soy sauce or tamari, remove from the heat, and cool. *(The carrot and mushroom salads can be prepared up to 2 days ahead. Transfer to separate food storage containers and refrigerate.)*

In a large bowl, massage the salad greens gently with a few drops of sesame oil. Divide the greens and rice among serving bowls. Top with the mushroom mixture and carrot mixture. Garnish with a soy egg and kimchi. Sprinkle with green onions and sesame seeds and serve with the dressing.

soy eggs

MAKES 4 EGGS

Soy eggs, popular in China, Korea, and Japan, are marinated hard-boiled, or nearly hard-boiled, eggs. The eggs can be made ahead, with longer-marinated eggs taking on more flavor and brown hue. I like the eggs when they're slightly jammy in the yolk, so I simmer for just five minutes, but if you prefer solid centers, allow the eggs to simmer a minute or two longer.

4 eggs

½ cup soy sauce or tamari

¼ cup warm water

2 tablespoons Chinese black vinegar or apple cider vinegar

1 tablespoon brown sugar

Fill a bowl with water and ice and set aside. Combine the eggs and enough water to cover in a small saucepan and bring to a simmer over medium heat. Stir gently and simmer for 5 minutes. Using a slotted spoon, transfer the eggs to the ice water and let stand until cool to the touch.

Meanwhile, combine the soy sauce or tamari, warm water, vinegar, and sugar in a small bowl. Carefully peel the eggs and submerge into the soy sauce mixture. (It might be necessary to place a small dish atop the eggs to submerge completely.) Refrigerate the eggs for at least 2 hours or up to 2 days.

Note: The soy egg marinade can be used more than once. Reserve it in a jar in the refrigerator for one or two more batches of eggs.

potato salad, lettuce cups, herb gribiche

4 SERVINGS / GF

Gribiche is a classic French sauce made thick and creamy with hard-boiled egg yolks. This version is chunky and not emulsified but stays true and tart with the traditional additions of mustard, cornichons, and capers. It's a most delicious way to turn potato salad into a main dish.

1½ pounds small waxy potatoes

Salt

Gribiche

½ cup olive oil

⅓ cup whole-grain Dijon mustard

⅓ cup white wine vinegar

12 cornichons (gherkins), thinly sliced

3 tablespoons drained capers

6 hard-boiled eggs, peeled, quartered, and sliced

Salad

3 cups sliced celery

½ small red onion, sliced

½ cup fresh Italian parsley leaves

Freshly cracked black pepper

Lettuce leaves, to line plates (optional)

Place the potatoes in a steamer set over a pot of rapidly boiling water and sprinkle lightly with salt. Cover and steam the potatoes until tender when pierced with a thin, sharp knife, about 20 minutes. Remove from the steamer and cool completely.

For the gribiche: In a medium bowl, whisk together the oil, mustard, vinegar, cornichons, and capers to blend. Gently mix in the eggs.

For the salad: Combine the celery, onion, and parsley in a large bowl. Peel and slice the potatoes into the bowl. Add the dressing, season the salad with pepper, and toss.

Arrange lettuce leaves on plates, if desired, and top with the salad to serve.

eggplant caponata, ricotta salata, celery leaves

4 SERVINGS / GF

You might be tempted to skip the salting of the eggplant, but don't. The salting process changes the texture of the eggplant—it becomes less spongy and therefore doesn't soak up a truckload of oil when you fry it. Ricotta salata is a firm, salty-sweet cheese that you can find at cheese stores, Italian markets, and Italian delis. (It's worth the hunt!) It's drier and less creamy than feta, but you can substitute feta in a pinch.

1 eggplant (1 to 1¼ pounds), cut into ½-inch dice

2 teaspoons salt

2 tablespoons extra-virgin olive oil, plus more for frying and drizzling

1½ cups diced celery (about 4 well-trimmed stalks)

1 medium red onion, diced

1 tablespoon honey

1 cup strained tomato puree (passata)

¼ cup white wine vinegar

¼ cup golden raisins

10 Castelvetrano olives, pitted and sliced

3 tablespoons capers

Pinch of red pepper flakes, or 1 dried arbol chile, stemmed, seeds shaken out, and crumbled

4 to 6 ounces ricotta salata, thinly sliced

1 cup baby or wild arugula

1 celery stalk, very thinly sliced on a diagonal

Celery leaves

Fresh mint leaves

Spread the eggplant pieces out on a sheet pan, sprinkle with the salt, and let stand for 30 minutes. Rinse and drain the eggplant, then blot dry on a tea towel.

Heat a thin layer of oil in a heavy large skillet over medium-high heat. Working in batches and adding more oil as needed, fry the eggplant, stirring occasionally, until golden brown and tender, about 7 minutes. Using a slotted spoon, transfer the eggplant to a bowl.

In the same skillet, heat the 2 tablespoons oil over medium-high heat. Add the celery and onion and sauté until beginning to soften, about 5 minutes. Increase the heat to high, drizzle the honey over the onion and celery, and cook until caramelized bits appear but the celery is still crunchy, about 2 minutes. Add the tomato puree, vinegar, raisins, olives, and capers and simmer until slightly thickened, about 2 minutes. Stir in the eggplant and red pepper flakes. Cool completely. *(The caponata can be made ahead and stored, covered, in the refrigerator for up to 6 days.)*

Divide the caponata among plates. Top with the ricotta salata. Scatter the salads with the arugula, celery, celery leaves, and mint leaves. Drizzle with oil, if desired, and serve.

chinese "no" chicken salad

4 SERVINGS / GF OPTION, VEGAN OPTION

The ever-popular Chinese chicken salad is not Chinese. Wolfgang Puck created it for his Chinois restaurant in Santa Monica in the '70s. This is my veggie version. Deep-frying rice noodles makes them puffy, and they add delicious crunch to the salad.

Dressing

¼ cup plus 2 tablespoons rice vinegar

¼ cup soy sauce or tamari

⅓ cup peanut, untoasted (light) sesame, or other neutral oil

3 tablespoons toasted sesame oil

2 tablespoons honey or agave nectar

2 teaspoons mustard powder

1 garlic clove, grated or pressed with a garlic press

½ teaspoon tangerine zest

Salad

6 cups (¼-inch-thick crosswise slices) napa cabbage (about 1 small head)

6 cups mixed greens, such as tatsoi, mizuna, and baby bok choy

6 small tangerines, peeled and separated into sections, or 3 oranges, peeled, halved, and thinly sliced

5 ounces sugar snap or snow peas, thinly sliced on a diagonal (about 1⅓ cups)

1 cup frozen shelled edamame, thawed

1 cup chopped celery

4 green onions, thinly sliced

½ cup chopped fresh cilantro

Peanut oil or other neutral oil, for frying

2 ounces rice stick noodles (mai fun), broken into 2- to 3-inch pieces

1 cup slivered almonds, toasted

¼ cup toasted sesame seeds, plus additional for sprinkling

Cilantro sprigs

For the dressing: Whisk together all the ingredients to blend in a small bowl. (*The salad dressing can be prepared up to 2 days ahead; cover and refrigerate.*)

For the salad: Combine the cabbage, mixed greens, tangerines, peas, edamame, celery, green onions, and cilantro in a very large bowl. (*The salad can be prepared to this point up to 1 day ahead; cover and refrigerate.*)

Heat 1 inch of peanut oil in a heavy medium skillet over high heat until almost smoking. Add one-quarter of the noodles to the hot oil and fry until the noodles puff, about 10 seconds. Using tongs, carefully turn the noodles in the pan over, if necessary, to fry on the other side. Transfer the fried noodles to a paper towel–lined pan to drain. Repeat with the remaining noodles in three batches.

Add the noodles, almonds, and sesame seeds to the bowl with the salad. Whisk the dressing to blend and pour it over the salad. Toss the salad with the dressing to coat. Divide the salad among plates and sprinkle with additional sesame seeds. Garnish with cilantro sprigs and serve.

indonesian gado-gado salad, spicy peanut sauce

4 TO 6 SERVINGS / GF OPTION

Gado-gado is an Indonesian vegetable dish that's made many ways. On some islands in the archipelago, it's a salad of crunchy raw vegetables; elsewhere, it's a steamed veggie plate, but it always features a rich peanut sauce. *Gado-gado* loosely translates to "hodgepodge," so feel free to riff on this classic by replacing the long beans with green beans, use kale for cabbage, etc. The crispy fried onions are the same ones that top holiday green bean casserole—crispy fried shallots are more authentic but the fried onions make a tasty and easy-to-find option.

Potatoes and Green Beans

Salt

12 ounces waxy potatoes, about 3 inches in diameter

1 bunch long beans (about 12 ounces), or 12 ounces green beans, trimmed and cut into 2-inch lengths

Slaw

3 cups mixed thinly sliced cabbages (such as savoy, green, napa, and red)

2 cups bean sprouts (soy or mung)

2 medium carrots, cut into julienne strips

3 green onions, very thinly sliced

Gado-Gado

3 tablespoons peanut oil

1 generous teaspoon ground turmeric

Salt and freshly ground black pepper

1 tablespoon fresh lime juice

4 hard-boiled eggs, peeled and quartered

1 pickling cucumber, cut in half lengthwise and thinly sliced on a diagonal

Purchased crispy fried shallots or onions

Chopped roasted peanuts (optional)

Spicy Coconut Peanut Sauce (page 218)

For the potatoes and green beans: Bring a large saucepan of salted water to a boil. Add the potatoes and cook until tender when pierced with a knife, about 14 minutes. Remove the potatoes with a slotted spoon to drain; maintain the boiling water. Add the long beans to the water and boil until just tender, about 4 minutes. Drain well.

For the slaw: Combine the cabbage, bean sprouts, carrots, and green onions in a large bowl. *(The slaw, potatoes, and green beans can be prepared up to 1 day ahead; cover separately and refrigerate.)*

For the gado-gado: Slice the potatoes into ¼-inch-thick rounds. Heat 2 tablespoons of the oil in a heavy large skillet over medium-high heat. Add the potatoes, sprinkle with the turmeric, and season with salt and pepper. Cook, turning once or twice, until golden brown on both sides, about 5 minutes. Remove from the heat and cool.

Toss the slaw with the long beans, the remaining 1 tablespoon peanut oil, and the lime juice. Top with the potatoes. Arrange the eggs and cucumber slices attractively atop the salad and sprinkle with fried shallots and peanuts, if desired. Serve with spicy coconut peanut sauce.

salade provençal panisse, lemon-chèvre dressing

4 SERVINGS / GF

We tend to think of Niçoise salad as a mix of tuna, eggs, olives, tomatoes, cooked potatoes, and green beans, but if you dive a little deeper, you learn that the salad evolved from a simple medley of vegetables that was eaten by fishermen with the day's catch after returning from the sea. I like to think of this sunny Provençal mélange as a post-harvest repast for gardeners. *Mesclun* is Provençal patois for "mix," and here it's a mix of whatever lettuces you have fresh and on hand. Panisse, chickpea fritters popular in the South of France, fry up crisp in olive oil to round out the meal, and a silken goat cheese dressing brings it all together beautifully. Pour a crisp dry rosé.

Dressing

4 ounces soft fresh goat cheese

½ cup extra-virgin olive oil

½ teaspoon lemon zest

6 tablespoons fresh lemon juice

2 green onions, sliced

2 large garlic cloves, peeled

1 tablespoon Dijon mustard

½ teaspoon salt

Salad

1 (6.7-ounce) package steamed artichoke hearts, or 1 (12-ounce) jar marinated grilled artichoke hearts, drained

2 celery stalks, thinly sliced

8 mini bell peppers, stemmed and sliced

1 small zucchini, thinly sliced

½ medium red onion, sliced

8 cups mesclun mix, such as arugula, spinach, baby romaine, dandelion greens, escarole, and radicchio

¼ cup fresh basil leaves

2 tablespoons fresh Italian parsley leaves (optional)

Extra-virgin olive oil, for drizzling

Salt

4 hard-boiled eggs, peeled and cut in half

2 medium tomatoes, preferably heirloom, cut into wedges

Olives, such as Niçoise, Lucques, oil-cured black, or picholine

Panisse (recipe follows)

For the dressing: Combine all the ingredients in a blender and blend until smooth. (*The dressing can be made up to 1 week ahead; cover and refrigerate. If made ahead, allow to come to room temperature before serving. If the dressing breaks, whir briefly in a blender.*)

For the salad: In a medium bowl, combine the artichoke hearts, celery, bell peppers, zucchini, and red onion with ½ cup of the dressing and let stand for 1 hour at room temperature or refrigerate for up to 8 hours.

recipe continues

When ready to serve: Combine the mesclun, basil, and parsley in a large bowl. Add a small drizzle of olive oil (about 2 teaspoons) and a sprinkle of salt. Using your hands, gently massage the greens mixture until very lightly coated but not bruised. Add the marinated vegetables and toss just to combine. Divide the salad among four plates. Top with the eggs, tomatoes, and olives. Scatter the salads with freshly fried panisse. Drizzle with the remaining dressing and serve.

panisse

These fritters are so tasty when dipped into the lemon–goat cheese dressing, you may be tempted to skip the salad. The addition of herbes de Provence, while not traditional, is quite tasty.

2 tablespoons extra-virgin olive oil, plus more for brushing and frying

1 cup chickpea (garbanzo bean) flour, preferably Bob's Red Mill

½ teaspoon salt

¼ teaspoon herbes de Provence or dried thyme

2 cups water

2 garlic cloves, finely grated or pressed with a garlic press

½ teaspoon finely grated lemon zest

Brush a 9 x 5-inch loaf pan with oil. Line the bottom and long sides of the pan with parchment paper, leaving an inch or two overhanging the sides; brush the parchment with oil.

In a medium saucepan, stir together the chickpea flour, salt, and herbes de Provence to blend. Gradually whisk in the water, garlic, lemon zest, and oil, breaking up any clumps. Set the pan over medium-high heat and stir with a wooden spoon until the mixtures thickens and bubbles. Reduce the heat to low and stir until the mixture is very thick and no longer tastes like raw beans, about 3 minutes. Immediately transfer to the prepared pan and, working quickly, spread to fill the pan evenly. Cool completely to set. *(The panisse can be prepared up to 4 days ahead. Cover and refrigerate.)*

Using the overhanging parchment as an aid, carefully remove the chickpea loaf. Cut the loaf crosswise into ½-inch-thick strips. Heat ½ inch of oil in a heavy medium skillet over medium-high heat until almost smoking. Fry the panisse until golden brown on both sides, turning once, about 3 minutes total.

tostada salad,
creamy lime-avocado dressing

6 SERVINGS / GF

My mother made taco salad for dinner a lot in the summer. We'd gather outside at a square picnic table underneath a massive hot-pink bougainvillea and towering palm tree and happily dig into her crunchy, creamy, cool, and crisp concoction. In my updated "tostada" version, there's no ground beef or grated cheddar, but the results are equally joy-inducing. If you are pressed for time, you can use 3 cups best-quality purchased tortilla chips instead of the freshly fried. Queso fresco is a crumbly cow's-milk cheese with a mild flavor that's available at most supermarkets.

6 corn tortillas

Corn oil or peanut oil, for frying

Salt

8 cups mixed greens, such as baby kale, baby gem, romaine hearts, and purslane, torn into bite-sized pieces if necessary

12 ounces jicama (about ½ medium), peeled and cut into ½ x 2-inch pieces

1 bunch radishes, trimmed and sliced

12 to 16 ounces cherry tomatoes, cut in half

1 (15-ounce) can black beans, rinsed and drained

½ red onion, chopped

Creamy Lime-Avocado Dressing (recipe follows)

8 ounces queso fresco, crumbled

½ cup chopped fresh cilantro

2 ripe but firm avocados, cut into chunks

Stack the tortillas and cut them in half. Cut the halved tortillas crosswise into ¾-inch-wide strips. Fill a heavy deep skillet with 1 inch of oil and heat over medium-high heat until very hot. Reduce the heat to medium, then, working in batches, add the tortilla pieces to the oil and fry, turning once, until the tortillas are golden and crisp, about 1 minute. Transfer the tortillas to a brown paper bag or paper towels to drain. Sprinkle the tortillas strips with salt. *(The tortillas strips can be made up to 8 hours ahead. Cover loosely and store at room temperature.)*

In a large bowl, combine the greens, jicama, radishes, cherry tomatoes, black beans, and red onion in a large bowl. Add the tortilla chips and enough dressing to suit your taste and toss to combine. Sprinkle the salad with the cheese and cilantro. Garnish with the avocado and serve.

recipe continues

creamy lime-avocado dressing

MAKES ABOUT 2½ CUPS

I often make a double batch of this thick and creamy dressing because it's so good as a dip for crudités and chips.

1 large avocado, sliced

1 cup chopped fresh cilantro

1 cup pepitas (shelled pumpkin seeds), toasted

⅔ cup extra-virgin olive oil

⅔ cup fresh lime juice

2 jalapeño chiles, stemmed and seeded

2 garlic cloves, peeled

1 teaspoon salt

Combine all the ingredients in a blender and blend until smooth. *(The dressing can be prepared up to 1 day ahead. Cover and refrigerate. Thin the dressing with additional lime juice and olive oil before using, if necessary.)*

PERFECT AVOCADOS

Finding ripe avocados at the market is about as rare as winning the lottery. The avocado display usually offers up just two choices: the rock-hard kind, or the mushy, guaranteed-to-be-stringy kind. A perfect avocado yields slightly from the gentlest amount of pressure applied by your fingers when held in the palm of your hand. These are the avocados that peel and pit easily and make picture-pretty slices that are tender and creamy to the bite.

As a native Californian who grew up eating mashed, seasoned avocado on toast before it was a "thing," I take pride in always having ripe avocados when I want them. It took years of picking up tips about how to buy, ripen, and store the beloved fruit (yes, it's a fruit!) from avocado growers, lucky owners of prolific backyard trees, vendors, and friends to get this delicious, nutrient-and-monounsaturated-fat-dense, perfectly-ready-avocado point.

I buy avocados weekly at my farmers' market or at the supermarket. Avocados from the farmers' market taste better to me—giant Reed's and Pinkertons are like gold, but you can't beat a Hass for year-round reliability. I choose extra-firm avocados and once home, I place them in a bowl and wait. As soon as the avocados begin to ripen but before they're quite ready, I move them to the refrigerator. The day before I want to enjoy one, I set it on the counter, and the next day, perfection is delivered. You can "hold off" ripening in the refrigerator for days, even weeks, once the avocado has begun to ripen.

To slice your ripened-to-perfection treat, use a small, sharp knife to cut the avocado in half lengthwise. With the tip of the same knife, carefully "pick" the pit up and out, always cutting away from your hand and not into it. I like to remove the peel with my fingers for unblemished slices, but if the peel stubbornly adheres to the flesh or if I plan to mash the avocado, I'll use a spoon to scoop out the pale, yellow-green meat instead. Once cut, a half avocado can be stored in the refrigerator for a day or two. To keep it from browning, run the cut side under cold water to moisten, then cover it with a waxed-fabric food wrapper.

44   VEGETARIAN SALAD FOR DINNER

baby gem, hearts of palm, avocado, radish, marcona almonds, green goddess

2 SERVINGS / GF

Hearts of palm and Green Goddess dressing have a retro, white-tablecloth-and-red-leather-booth vibe, but the two old-school salad stars are still great, especially together. Hearts of palm are a good source of lean protein, fiber, vitamins, and minerals, and zippy Green Goddess, redolent with herbs and lemon, is having a big culinary comeback. The two combine deliciously in this light supper.

2 heads baby gem lettuce

1 large avocado, sliced

1 (14-ounce) can young hearts of palm, drained, patted dry, and thickly sliced

2 medium-small watermelon radishes, thinly sliced with a V-slicer

About ⅔ cup Green Goddess Dressing (recipe follows)

⅓ cup Marcona almonds

Freshly cracked black pepper

Trim the bottoms of the lettuce heads. Separate the leaves and arrange on two plates. Top with the avocado, hearts of palm, and radish slices. Spoon the dressing over the salads and sprinkle with the almonds. Season with pepper and serve.

green goddess dressing

MAKES ABOUT 2 CUPS

Created in San Francisco in the '20s, this dressing has stood the test of time. It was my favorite bottled dressing as a kid, and now it's my spring go-to for salads, crudités, and sandwiches. Traditionally, anchovies give the dressing its round, salty edge, but capers make an excellent vegetarian replacement. I've included the anchovy option for purists. Either way, this recipe makes enough to dress the salad with extra to enjoy later.

1 cup sour cream

½ cup fresh lemon juice

½ cup mayonnaise

½ cup snipped fresh chives (about 1 bunch)

½ cup fresh tarragon leaves

3 garlic cloves, peeled

2 scant tablespoons capers or chopped anchovy fillets

1 teaspoon salt, or more to taste

Freshly ground black pepper

Combine the sour cream, lemon juice, mayonnaise, chives, tarragon, garlic, capers or anchovies, and salt in a blender and blend until smooth. Season with additional salt, if necessary, and pepper. *(The dressing can be prepared up to 1 week ahead. Transfer to a jar and refrigerate.)*

lettuce cups, thai flavors, cauliflower tempeh

2 TO 4 SERVINGS / GF, VEGAN OPTION

I fell in love with Thai food as a teenager at a tiny strip mall restaurant. This was not all that long after famed chef Jet Tila's family opened the first Thai grocery in the US. I remember making trips to their Bangkok Market and wondering at the assortment of exotic ingredients. My first forays into Thai cooking were totally inauthentic in terms of preparation but had satisfying flavors owing to the availability of Thai ingredients at Bangkok Market. (Mind you, this was before the internet and the proliferation of English-language Thai cookbooks.) I still love creating dishes inspired by Thai flavors—like these lettuce cups with a chewy-crispy filling topped with cooling herbs.

1½ cups water

5 garlic cloves, finely grated or pressed with a garlic press

1½ teaspoons salt

1 (8-ounce) package tempeh

3 cups chopped cauliflower (¼- to ½-inch pieces; about ½ head)

½ cup minced shallot

¼ cup fresh lime juice

¼ cup fish sauce, vegan if desired

¼ cup lightly packed brown sugar

Bibb or green-leaf lettuce, to line a platter

⅓ cup peanut oil, untoasted (light) sesame oil, or other neutral oil

½ cup fresh mint leaves

2 garlic cloves, minced

1 small red Thai chile, thinly sliced

Mint sprigs

Cilantro sprigs (optional)

Lime wedges

In a medium bowl, stir together the water, garlic, and salt to blend. Cut the tempeh ½-inch-thick slices. Add the tempeh to the garlic water and soak for 30 minutes. Drain well, blot dry, and crumble into ½-inch pieces. Combine the tempeh, cauliflower, and shallots in a large bowl and set aside.

In a small bowl, stir together the lime juice, fish sauce, and brown sugar to blend. Line a large platter with lettuce leaves.

Heat the oil in a heavy very large skillet over high heat until very hot. Add the tempeh mixture and stir-fry until beginning to brown, about 6 minutes. Add the mint leaves, minced garlic, and chile and cook, stirring frequently, until the mixture is mostly well browned, about 6 minutes longer. Spoon the tempeh mixture onto the lettuce and garnish with mint and cilantro, if desired. Serve with the remaining sauce and lime wedges.

Ingredient note: To my palate, Thai-style lime dressing begs for Thai fish sauce. Vegan versions of fish sauce exist and are quite tasty, but I prefer the umami punch of the real deal. For more information about tempeh, see page 203.

vietnamese-style salad rolls, hoisin peanut sauce

MAKES 16 ROLLS, 4 TO 8 SERVINGS / GF, V

I first ate Vietnamese rice paper rolls (gỏi cuốn) in Paris as a high school exchange student. At the time I had only ever eaten a fried egg roll, and the fresh, herbal, rice paper–encased "salad" revealed a whole new world of flavor to me. Making salad rolls can be a chore, but they make for a great interactive dinner—gather a few friends around a table spread with all the fixings and have your guests roll their own. They'll thank you.

2 ounces rice stick noodles (mai fun)

1 head butter lettuce

2 cups julienne strips of carrot (about 3 carrots)

1 hothouse cucumber, cut into 3-inch-long, ½-inch-wide, and ⅛-inch-thick slices (about 2 cups)

1 (7-ounce) package sriracha- or teriyaki-flavored baked tofu, cut into 32 thin strips

32 large fresh basil leaves

64 fresh mint leaves

1 cup fresh cilantro leaves

1 bunch garlic chives, cut into 3-inch-long pieces, or 2 green onions, cut into 3-inch-long, ⅛-inch-thick slices

16 to 32 fresh perilla or shiso leaves

16 round rice paper spring roll wrappers (bánh tráng)

Hoisin Peanut Sauce (recipe follows)

Bring a medium saucepan of water to a simmer over high heat. Add the noodles and boil until tender, about 3 minutes. Drain and cover with cold water to cool. Drain the noodles well.

Line a tray with a clean, damp towel. Separate the lettuce into leaves. Carefully tear away the center rib, dividing each leaf into pieces. (Reserve the crisper center leaves for another use.) Fill a large bowl with warm water. Submerge one rice paper wrapper in water and let stand until it just begins to soften, about 30 seconds. Transfer the wrapper to a large clean work surface. Arrange 2 pieces of lettuce about 3 inches in from the bottom side (the part of the wrapper closest to you) and 1 inch from the rounded edges on each side. Top the lettuce with 2 tablespoons carrot, 2 tablespoons cucumber, 2 pieces of tofu, 2 basil leaves, 4 mint leaves, 1 tablespoon cilantro leaves, and a few garlic chives or green onions. Carefully arrange the perilla leaves over the vegetable mixture. Top the perilla leaves about ¼ cup of the noodles. Fold the bottom edge of the wrapper up over the vegetable mixture; fold the sides of the wrapper in over the vegetable mixture to enclose. Carefully roll the wrapper around the fillings into a neat, tight bundle. Transfer to the prepared tray. Cover the rolls with another clean, damp towel and repeat the process with the remaining wrappers and ingredients; keep the finished rolls covered with the damp towel as you work and until you're ready to serve them. *(The salad rolls can be made up to 6 hours ahead. Cover the tray with plastic wrap or foil and refrigerate.)*

Serve the rolls with the sauce.

hoisin peanut sauce

MAKES ABOUT 2 GENEROUS CUPS

Any leftover peanut sauce can be used as a spicy-sweet dressing for shredded cabbage or cold noodles or as a dip for crudités.

½ cup hoisin sauce (gluten-free, if desired)

1 cup water, plus more if needed

1 large shallot, minced

2 garlic cloves, minced

¾ cup smooth unsweetened peanut butter

1 to 2 tablespoons sambal oelek

2 tablespoons fresh lime juice

½ cup roasted peanuts, chopped (optional)

Bring the hoisin sauce, water, shallot, and garlic to a boil in a heavy medium saucepan over medium-high heat; lower the heat and simmer for 1 minute. Add the peanut butter and 1 tablespoon of the sambal oelek and whisk until smooth. Remove the sauce from the heat. Add the lime juice, remaining sambal oelek to taste, and more water to thin the sauce to a dipping consistency. Transfer to a bowl and cool completely. *(The sauce can be prepared up to 1 week ahead; cover and refrigerate.)*

Stir the peanuts into the sauce just before serving, if desired.

HOISIN SAUCE

Hoisin sauce is a Chinese cooking sauce and condiment made from fermented soybeans, spices, garlic and sugar. Like other products made from fermented soybeans, it is an excellent way to add umami to vegetarian dishes. Although a little harder to find, gluten-free hoisin is available. The dark, salty-sweet sauce is vegan, even though *hoisin* means "seafood" in Cantonese.

greek salad, greek fava dip

4 SERVINGS / GF

Greek fava is a comforting and rib-sticking yellow pea dip. The name is a little confusing, as there are both fresh and dried fava beans, some of which are yellow, but Greek fava is indeed made with yellow split peas (not fava beans!). I serve this fava with another Greek classic, the ever-popular Greek salad. While I have been making and loving said salad for years, it wasn't until I took a trip to Greece that I learned that traditionally, there is no lettuce in the mix and that the elements are mostly served up in large chunks. The key to the silkiest fava dip is thoroughly cooked yellow peas. Try to purchase the yellow split peas from a quality grocer where you can be assured that the beans are fresh. Dried beans and pulses that have been sitting on the shelf for years take a very long time to soften. An Instant Pot is a handy tool for cooking the yellow peas—I've included instructions for doing so.

Fava Dip

1 cup (8 ounces) yellow split peas or chana dal

¼ cup plus 2 tablespoons extra-virgin olive oil

1 yellow onion, sliced

5 garlic cloves, sliced

4 cups water

1 teaspoon dried oregano

½ teaspoon red pepper flakes

½ teaspoon salt, or to taste

Salad

6 small tomatoes, cored and cut into wedges

2 hothouse cucumbers, or 6 Persian cucumbers, halved lengthwise and thickly sliced on a diagonal

12 mini bell peppers, stemmed and sliced

1 small to medium red onion, cut into thin wedges

½ cup pitted kalamata olives

Oregano Vinaigrette (recipe follows)

8 ounces feta cheese, cut into ¾-inch-thick slices

Extra-virgin olive oil, for drizzling

2 tablespoons capers

Dried oregano, for crumbling

For the fava: Soak the split peas in a medium bowl covered in a few inches of water overnight. Drain.

To cook the peas on the stovetop: Heat ¼ cup of the oil in a heavy large saucepan over medium heat. Add the onion and sauté until translucent and beginning to color, about 10 minutes. Stir in the garlic. Add the split peas, water, oregano, and red pepper flakes and bring to a simmer over medium heat. Reduce the heat to low, cover, and simmer until the peas are very tender and losing their shape, about 1½ hours. Uncover the peas and simmer, stirring frequently, until the mixture has reduced to 3 cups, about 15 minutes. Cool.

recipe continues

To cook the peas in an Instant Pot: Cook the onion in the ¼ cup oil on Sauté mode until tender, about 10 minutes. Add the drained peas and the garlic and stir to coat with oil. Stir in 2½ cups water, the oregano, and the red pepper flakes. Seal and cook on Bean mode, then allow the pressure to release naturally. Return the Instant Pot to Sauté mode and cook, stirring frequently, until the mixture has reduced to 3 cups, about 20 minutes.

Transfer the pea mixture to the food processor. Add the remaining 2 tablespoons oil and ½ teaspoon salt and puree until smooth. Add additional salt to taste. *(The dip can be prepared up to 5 days ahead; cover and refrigerate. Allow the fava to stand briefly at room temperature before serving to remove the chill and bring out the flavor.)*

For the salad: Gently toss the tomatoes, cucumber, bell peppers, red onion, and olives in a medium bowl with enough oregano vinaigrette to coat generously. Let stand for 1 hour.

To serve: Divide the dip among plates. Using the back of a spoon, spread the dip into a ¾-inch-thick round in the center of each plate. Spoon the salad around the dip. Top the salad and dip with cheese and drizzle with additional vinaigrette. Sprinkle with the capers and oregano and serve.

oregano vinaigrette

MAKES ABOUT 1¼ CUPS

¾ cup extra-virgin olive oil

½ cup red wine vinegar

2 garlic cloves, finely grated or pressed with a garlic press

½ teaspoon dried oregano, crumbled

½ teaspoon salt, or more to taste

¼ teaspoon red pepper flakes

Freshly cracked black pepper

Whisk together the oil, vinegar, garlic, oregano, salt, and red pepper flakes to blend in a medium bowl or shake in a covered jar. Season with cracked black pepper and additional salt. *(The dressing can be made up to 3 days ahead. Cover and refrigerate.)*

grain salads

Whole grains are healthy, versatile, comforting, and satisfying. Bulgur, barley, farro, freekeh, and brown rice are nutritious whole grains that become the centerpiece of or sidekick to these hearty salads. Everyday and heirloom grains become uncommon and modern dinner salads.

Bulgur, aka cracked wheat, is familiar to people from tabbouleh, the popular Levantine parsley, herb, and tomato salad. Bulgur cooks in a minute and has a way of soaking up dressing without becoming mushy or dry. It's an easy, wheaty-tasting salad grain. Freekeh, also from the Levant, is green wheat that's burned as part of the harvest process, giving it a slight smoky flavor.

Barley is one of the oldest cultivated grains, and it is popular worldwide. The barley used for these salads is pearled. Pearling refers to the removal of the husk, allowing for a shorter cooking time. Maybe it's because my mom used lots of barley in her thick soups that I think of it as a very comforting grain. The barley salads here—a warm salad with creamy wild mushrooms and a slightly sweet salad with lots of sesame and tenderized kale—are just that.

Farro, semi-pearled wheat berries, tastes good simply simmered and dressed with a little salt and olive oil—and it's hard to overcook. Farro is a personal favorite—it's flavorful, forgiving, and flexible. Farro can shine when embellished with a few herbs and a vinaigrette, and adds taste and texture to a green salad.

Rice is the world's most widely consumed grain, accounting for a major portion of humanity's calories. There are many varieties of rice, each with its own subtle flavor. I remember a time not long ago when the selection at the supermarket consisted of white and brown long-grain rice. Now it's common to find many different types—red, pink, black, jasmine, basmati, short-grain, medium-grain, and long-grain. Wild rice, a close relative to cultivated rice, is an indigenous grain with a greener, grassier flavor.

Not every grain grown is represented in the following section: I use the ones that I think make the best salads.

carrot, bulgur, green olives, arugula, date, preserved lemon

4 SERVINGS / VEGAN OPTION

This salad is a perfect example of Cal-Med cooking—a blend of farmers' market carrots, arugula, and healthy bulgur with all the right notes; tart-bright lemon, savory-salty olives, and rich-sweet dates. This is one of my favorite lunchtime meals. The salad is adaptable—if you don't have preserved lemons on hand, you can add additional lemon juice; if you want to add extra protein, you can crumble on some feta cheese.

Salt

¾ cup quick-cooking medium-grain bulgur wheat

1 pound tender carrots, sliced

6 tablespoons extra-virgin olive oil

1 garlic clove, finely grated or crushed with a garlic press

½ cup chopped pitted green olives, such as Castelvetrano or Cerignola

⅓ cup chopped Preserved Lemon (page 218)

2 green onions, sliced

4 cups wild arugula

2 ounces (or more) crumbled feta cheese (optional)

⅓ cup sliced pitted Deglet Noor dates

¼ cup fresh lemon juice, or more to taste

Aleppo pepper

Lemon wedges

Bring a large pot of salted water to a boil. Add the bulgur and cook for 2 minutes. Add the carrots and boil until the carrots are just becoming tender, 2 to 3 minutes. Drain well and transfer to a large bowl. Stir in 2 tablespoons of the oil and the garlic and cool completely.

Mix in the olives, preserved lemon, and green onions. *(The salad can be prepared up to this point up to 1 day ahead. Cover and refrigerate.)*

Stir in the arugula, cheese, if desired, and dates along with the remaining ¼ cup oil and the lemon juice. Season with Aleppo pepper and serve with lemon wedges.

grape (or plum), fennel, tabbouleh, goat cheese "cream," saba

4 TO 6 SERVINGS / VEGAN OPTION

This take on tabbouleh, the bulgur, tomato, and parsley salad popular in the Levant region, is a subtler, sweeter blend of cracked wheat, fresh fruit, vegetables, and herbs. Juicy grapes form a bridge to the saba, a grape must reduction from Italy that has just the right hint of sweetness. Saba can be tricky to find (look for it at Italian specialty foods stores), but grape molasses from Middle Eastern markets and concentrated balsamic vinegar are good for the drizzle too. When I have ripe plums, I'll make the salad with plums or plums and grapes. Note that the goat cheese cream is suitable for most folks with cow's-milk or lactose intolerances, and vegans can try my Cashew Cream (page 214).

1 cup quick-cooking medium-grain bulgur wheat

1 cup boiling water

8 ounces soft fresh goat cheese

¾ cup milk, such as goat's, cow's, or unsweetened seed or nut milk

3 cups halved red grapes or diced pitted red plums, or a mix

1 large or 2 small fennel bulbs, trimmed and chopped

1 cup coarsely chopped fresh Italian parsley leaves

½ cup finely chopped red onion

⅓ cup extra-virgin olive oil, plus more for drizzling

¼ cup fresh lemon juice

½ teaspoon salt

Saba, grape molasses, or extra-fancy balsamic vinegar, for drizzling

Chopped pistachios (optional)

Fennel fronds and/or fennel pollen, for garnish (optional)

Place the bulgur in a large bowl. Pour over the boiling water and let stand until all the water has been absorbed, about 1 hour.

Meanwhile, stir together the cheese and milk in a medium bowl until smooth.

Add the grapes, fennel, parsley, onion, oil, lemon juice, and salt to the bulgur in the bowl and stir to combine. (The cream and tabbouleh can be made up to 3 days ahead. Cover separately and refrigerate.)

Spoon the tabbouleh onto a platter or plates. Top with the goat cheese cream and drizzle with saba, grape molasses, or balsamic vinegar. Sprinkle with pistachios, if desired. Garnish with fennel fronds and/or pollen, if desired, and serve.

sweet sesame barley, kale, tofu

6 SERVINGS / VEGAN

Toasted sesame, fresh ginger, and a hint of soy sauce are what gives this hearty barley and kale do-ahead salad a Japanese influence. Tahini makes the vegan dressing rich and creamy. I like to add cubes of purchased baked teriyaki tofu for extra protein, but the salad is tasty without the addition of tofu too.

Dressing

½ cup rice vinegar

⅓ cup tahini (sesame seed paste)

3 tablespoons toasted sesame oil

2 tablespoons untoasted (light) sesame oil or extra-virgin olive oil

3 tablespoons brown sugar

2½ tablespoons soy sauce or tamari

1 tablespoon grated peeled fresh ginger

2 garlic cloves, finely grated or crushed with a garlic press

Salad

1 tablespoon toasted sesame oil

1 cup pearled barley

3½ cups water

½ teaspoon salt, or more to taste

8 cups lightly packed bite-sized pieces kale leaves

2 green onions, sliced

1 (6- to 7-ounce) package baked teriyaki-flavored tofu, cut into ½-inch cubes

3 tablespoons toasted sesame seeds

Freshly ground black pepper

For the dressing: Whisk together all the ingredients to blend in a medium bowl. *(The dressing can be prepared up to 4 days ahead; cover and refrigerate.)*

For the salad: Heat the oil in a heavy medium saucepan over medium-high heat. Add the barley and stir until lightly toasted, about 3 minutes. Add the water and salt and bring to a boil. Reduce the heat to medium-low and simmer until the barley is tender, about 40 minutes. Cool completely. *(The barley can be prepared up to 3 days ahead. Cover and refrigerate.)*

Combine the barley, kale, and green onions in a large bowl. Add the dressing and toss to combine. Mix in the tofu, if desired, and sesame seeds and season with salt and pepper. Cover and refrigerate the salad to allow the kale to soften slightly and the flavors to develop, about 1 hour. *(The salad can be made up to 1 day ahead. Keep refrigerated.)*

pink rice, long bean, lime leaf, fresh turmeric, sambal egg

6 SERVINGS / GF OPTION

I have had the good fortune of visiting several of Indonesia's islands with my brother, who once lived there. On Sulawesi we tasted pink rice steamed in bamboo pipes, on Ambon I first saw what fresh turmeric looked like, on Java we ate curries infused with lime leaf, and on Sumatra we enjoyed eggs in sambal—the salsa of the Indonesian archipelago. Here's a bold and fragrant salad that pays tribute to all those lovely places and tastes. As some of the ingredients can be hard to find, I offer brown rice as a substitute for pink or red rice and lime zest as an alternative to the lime leaves. I do hesitate to recommend dried turmeric in place of fresh, as that flavor skews the dish in a different direction. Fresh turmeric is getting easier to find (they carry it at my local chain grocery store), as the health benefits of eating turmeric are becoming popular.

Dressing

¼ cup rice vinegar

4 (1-inch) pieces fresh turmeric, peeled

2 (1-inch) pieces fresh ginger, peeled

1 red Holland, Fresno, or jalapeño chile

2 tablespoons brown sugar

3 garlic cloves, peeled

½ teaspoon salt

½ cup untoasted (light) sesame oil or peanut oil

3 tablespoons fresh lime juice

Salad

Salt

1 bunch long beans (about 12 ounces), or 12 ounces green beans, trimmed and cut into 1- to 2-inch lengths

1½ cups pink, red, or brown rice

6 makrut lime leaves, or 1 generous teaspoon freshly grated lime zest

3 cups chopped cabbage

Fresh lime juice (optional)

Sambal Eggs (recipe follows), cut in half

For the dressing: Combine the vinegar, turmeric, ginger, chile, brown sugar, garlic, and salt in a blender and blend until the turmeric and ginger are pureed. Add the oil and lime juice and pulse to blend. *(The dressing can be prepared up to 4 days ahead; cover and refrigerate.)*

For the salad: Bring a large pot of salted water to a boil. Add the long beans and cook until just tender, about 4 minutes. Using a slotted spoon, transfer the beans to a colander and refresh under cold water. Drain well. Add the rice to the boiling water and cook until tender, about 35 minutes. Drain well. Transfer the rice to a large bowl and cool completely.

recipe continues

Peel away the stem and center rib from the lime leaves. Stack the lime leaves and, using a sharp knife, cut them into very fine slivers. Add the lime leaves to the rice mixture along with the long beans and cabbage. Pour over the dressing and toss to combine. Taste and add lime juice, if desired. Top with sambal eggs and serve.

Note: If you are running short on time, you can toss 6 hard-boiled eggs with 3 tablespoons purchased sambal oelek in place of making your own sambal eggs.

sambal eggs

MAKES 6 EGGS

Medan is not the prettiest place in Sumatra—it's a congested business center without much to tempt the tourist, but it's a necessary stopping point on the way to both glorious Lake Toba and the highland jungles where orangutans roam. In Medan, I overnighted in a homely business hotel that was memorable for two things: the thick clouds of tobacco smoke floating around courtesy of chain-smoking businessmen, and the exceptional breakfast buffet. A highlight of the spread was a rice porridge surrounded with bowls of toppings—crispy fried shallots, green onions, threads of lime leaf, fresh chile slices, sweet-sticky kecap manis (Indonesia's thick soy-type sauce), and hard-boiled eggs stewed in a fragrant sambal. Luckily only the memory of that impressive meal lingers, and not the smoke. This recipe is my attempt to re-create the eggs. Enjoy the eggs with the Pink Rice Salad or with fried rice.

7 red Holland chiles, stemmed and cut into 1-inch pieces

⅔ cup sliced shallots (about 2)

⅔ cup sliced tender lemongrass (from about 3 stalks)

3 large garlic cloves, peeled

3 tablespoons peanut oil, untoasted (light) sesame oil, or other neutral oil

2 tablespoons soy sauce or tamari

½ cup water

1 teaspoon brown sugar

½ teaspoon salt

6 hard-boiled eggs, peeled

Combine the chiles, shallots, lemongrass, and garlic in a food processor and process until finely chopped and mushy.

Heat the oil in a heavy medium skillet over medium-high heat. Add the chile mixture and sauté until it just begins to brown and stick at the edges, about 3 minutes. Reduce the heat to medium-low, add the soy sauce or tamari, and stir until the liquid has reduced a bit, about 1 minute. Add the water, brown sugar, and salt, bring to a simmer, and simmer until the sambal is tender and thickens slightly, about 4 minutes. Combine the eggs and sambal in a bowl or container large enough for the eggs to be completely immersed in the sambal. Cover and refrigerate overnight or for up to 2 days before serving.

black rice, snap peas, pea sprouts, black garlic tofu

2 TO 4 SERVINGS / GF OPTION, VEGAN

Black garlic results from very slow caramelization of garlic bulbs. Low, slow, moist heat applied for a few weeks turns garlic's sharp bite into soft, mellow sticky black cloves. The flavor is akin to garlicky caramel with balsamic notes. I knew the sweet funkiness of black garlic would take tofu from bland to elevated, and a quick internet search of "black garlic tofu" led me to a post on the blog *Feasting at Home*. There I discovered a technique that was so good, I adapted it to add to this salad of antioxidant-rich black rice and spring peas. For ease, I cook the rice in boiling water as one would cook pasta.

1 cup black rice (Forbidden Rice)

Salt

1 tablespoon toasted sesame oil

6 ounces snap peas, trimmed and thinly sliced on a diagonal

3 green onions, thinly sliced on a diagonal

3 tablespoons Chinese black vinegar or sherry vinegar

12 to 14 ounces extra-firm tofu, cut into ¾-inch-thick slices

1 head black garlic, peeled

3 tablespoons untoasted (light) sesame oil or peanut oil, plus 2 tablespoons for frying

2 tablespoons soy sauce or tamari

2 tablespoons water

1 tablespoon brown sugar

2 ounces pea sprouts

Bring a large pot of salted water to a rapid boil. Add the rice and boil until just tender, about 35 minutes. Drain well. Transfer the rice to a medium bowl; stir in the toasted sesame oil and cool completely. Stir in the snap peas, green onions, and 2 tablespoons of the vinegar. *(This can be done up to 8 hours ahead; cover and refrigerate.)*

Meanwhile, line a small sheet pan with a folded clean dish towel. Arrange the tofu slices in a single layer atop the towel. Place another towel over the tofu and gently press on the tofu to remove excess moisture. Cut the tofu into ¾-inch cubes and carefully set aside.

Mince the black garlic (it will mash a bit) and transfer it to a glass measuring cup. Add the 3 tablespoons untoasted sesame oil, the soy sauce or tamari, water, and brown sugar and whisk vigorously, breaking down the garlic. In a separate small bowl, whisk together 2 tablespoons of the black garlic mixture and the remaining 1 tablespoon black vinegar to make a vinaigrette.

recipe continues

When ready to serve: Spoon the rice salad onto a serving dish and top with pea sprouts. Drizzle the vinaigrette over the salad.

Heat the remaining 2 tablespoons untoasted sesame oil in a heavy large skillet over medium-high heat until very hot but not smoking. Carefully add the tofu and fry, turning and stirring carefully with a slotted spoon until browned on all sides, about 8 minutes. Transfer the tofu to a plate with the slotted spoon. Pour the black garlic mixture into the skillet and stir until the mixture bubbles. Working quickly, return the tofu to the skillet and toss just to coat, about 30 seconds. Spoon the tofu and any remaining black garlic sauce over the salad and serve.

BLACK RICE

Black rice is a variety of whole-grain rice, like brown rice yet much darker. The color comes from the same antioxidant pigment that makes berries and grapes dark, which means that black rice will also have similar antioxidant health benefits. There are over twenty different varieties of black rice, ranging from short to long grain. In China, the common variety is a medium-grain rice grown in the north known as Forbidden Rice because it was once reserved for the aristocracy. Forbidden Rice is very black and is an excellent rice for making salads. Another variety that is often available at local supermarkets is Black Pearl rice. It's a little less black than Forbidden Rice, and has a longer, firmer grain, but it's also good for salads. In my recipe for Black Rice Salad, I boil the rice as I would make pasta to account for the different varieties of black rice cooking times and starch levels. Pro-tip: Be careful to not spill any of the black rice grains in your kitchen when preparing a recipe. I am not alone in freaking out about an overnight mouse infestation before happily remembering last night's dinner.

crispy farro, winter greens, persimmon, pomegranate, hazelnuts

4 SERVINGS / VEGAN OPTION

Skillet flip-fried cooked farro is a crunchy, crisp addition to this festive jewel-toned salad. Toasted hazelnuts and a hazelnut oil dressing enhance the nutty flavor of the wheat berries, but the salad is excellent when made with walnuts and walnut oil too. I especially like to pair the salad with a soft-ripened goat cheese such as Cypress Grove's Humboldt Fog or a French bucheron.

1½ cups farro

Salt

Dressing

½ cup hazelnut oil

¼ cup Champagne or white wine vinegar

2 tablespoons honey or agave nectar

2 tablespoons minced shallot

½ teaspoon salt

Salad

4 tablespoons peanut or extra-virgin olive oil

Salt

4 generous cups lightly packed winter greens, such as radicchio, red mustard, Belgian endive, Treviso, arugula, or red-leaf lettuce

1 fennel bulb, trimmed and very thinly sliced

2 Fuyu persimmons, very thinly sliced

1 cup pomegranate seeds

¾ cup roasted or toasted hazelnuts, coarsely chopped

Boil the farro in a medium pot of rapidly boiling salted water until just tender, about 20 minutes. Drain well. Transfer to a bowl and cool completely. *(The farro can be cooked up to 5 days ahead; cover and refrigerate.)*

For the dressing: Whisk the ingredients to blend in a small bowl.

For the salad: Heat 2 tablespoons of the oil in a heavy large skillet over high heat. Add half the farro, sprinkle with salt, and fry until golden and crispy, flipping the farro occasionally with a spatula to avoid burning, about 6 minutes. Transfer the farro to a plate and repeat with the remaining 2 tablespoons oil and farro. Cool the farro to warm or room temperature.

Combine the greens, fennel, persimmon, and pomegranate seeds in a large bowl. Add the farro and hazelnuts. Toss the salad with enough dressing to coat and serve.

zucchini and freekeh salad with za'atar, halloumi

4 SERVINGS

Freekeh is a staple in the Levant region. The nutritious, smoky-tasting grain is harvested from young green wheat stalks that are fire-roasted in the fields. It's worth a trip to a Middle Eastern emporium to buy it, and while there, get the salty-squeaky Halloumi cheese, za'atar, and Aleppo pepper. You can make the salad with easy-to-find bulgur too. Serve it with summer's best tomatoes and nectarines.

Freekeh

1 tablespoon extra-virgin olive oil, plus more for brushing

1½ cups (about 9 ounces) freekeh (fire-roasted green wheat)

3 cups water

Generous pinch of salt

Dressing

3 tablespoons fresh lemon juice

3 tablespoons extra-virgin olive oil

1 tablespoon za'atar

1 garlic clove, finely grated or crushed with a garlic press

½ teaspoon Aleppo pepper

Salad

1½ pounds zucchini (about 3), trimmed and quartered lengthwise

Extra-virgin olive oil

Za'atar, for sprinkling

Salt

½ to 1 cup chopped fresh Italian parsley

2 green onions, sliced

3 tablespoons toasted sesame seeds

8 to 9 ounces Halloumi cheese

For the freekeh: Heat 1 tablespoon of the oil in a heavy saucepan over medium-high heat. Add the freekeh and stir until lightly toasted, about 3 minutes. Add the water and salt and bring to a boil. Reduce the heat to medium-low, cover, and simmer until the freekeh is tender and the liquid has been absorbed, about 25 minutes. Transfer the freekeh to a large bowl and cool to room temperature.

Meanwhile, prepare the dressing: Whisk together the lemon juice, oil, za'atar, garlic and Aleppo pepper in a small bowl to blend.

For the salad: Heat a grill to medium-high. Brush the zucchini with oil and sprinkle generously with za'atar. Sprinkle with salt and grill, turning occasionally, until browned and tender, about 15 minutes. Transfer to a cutting board and cool.

Cut the zucchini into 1-inch pieces and add to the freekeh along with the parsley, green onions, and sesame seeds.

When ready to serve: Heat a grill to medium. Slice the cheese into ½-inch-thick slices. Brush the cheese with oil and sprinkle generously with za'atar. Grill the cheese until golden brown, about 4 minutes on each side. Toss the salad with the dressing, top with the cheese, and sprinkle generously with additional za'atar.

summer succotash salad, herb dressing

6 TO 8 SERVINGS

As any gardener knows, there are times when your summer garden might yield just one or a handful of a variety of ready-to-pick vegetables. To make the best use of a varied yet limited harvest, I created this easily adaptable salad with the idea being that you could pick a few ripe tomatoes, green beans, cucumbers, zucchini, and peppers from your garden, CSA box, or crisper and mix them into a proper meal. The blended dressing, with a mix of summer herbs, makes more than you need for this recipe, but you'll love having extra to drizzle over grilled vegetables or summer tomatoes. Sweet corn transforms the salad into a succotash, and a new favorite at picnics and barbecues.

Dressing

1 cup extra-virgin olive oil

½ cup red wine vinegar

½ cup packed fresh basil leaves

½ cup packed fresh dill sprigs or mint leaves

½ cup packed fresh cilantro or Italian parsley sprigs

4 garlic cloves, peeled

1 teaspoon salt

Salad

4 ears fresh corn, or 1 pound frozen yellow corn kernels

1 cup farro or barley

Salt

1 pound green beans, cut into 2-inch pieces

8 ounces small zucchini (about 2), thinly sliced

1 red bell pepper, diced

1 small red onion, diced

1 pint cherry tomatoes, cut in half

1 small cucumber, diced

1 jalapeño chile, finely chopped

Additional fresh herbs, for garnish

8 ounces feta cheese, crumbled

For the dressing: Blend all the ingredients in a blender until smooth. *(The dressing can be made up to 4 days ahead. Cover and refrigerate.)*

For the salad: Using a large sharp knife, cut the corn kernels from the cobs. Place the fresh or frozen corn kernels in a large bowl.

Cook the farro in rapidly boiling salted water until tender, about 25 minutes. Drain the farro well and add it to the corn. Cook the green beans in a skillet of rapidly boiling salted water until crisp-tender, about 4 minutes. Drain well and add to the bowl with the farro. Let stand until the farro and green beans are cool and the corn is warmed or thawed. Add the zucchini, bell pepper, and red onion. Pour about half the dressing over the salad, season with cracked black pepper, and toss to combine. *(The salad can be made up to this point up to 1 day ahead.)*

Add the tomatoes, cucumber, and jalapeño to the salad and toss to combine. Add additional dressing to taste and sprinkle with herbs. Serve, passing the crumbled cheese separately.

brussels sprouts, wild rice, ancho-spiced pecans, dates, goat cheese

2 TO 4 SERVINGS / GF

Wild rice is technically a grass, but when tossed with roasted Brussels sprouts, sweet-spiced pecans, and dates into a fall salad, it doesn't matter what it is because it's hearty, full-flavored, and very tasty. Make this salad part of your Thanksgiving feast and everyone, vegetarian or not, will thank you. You can find the ancho chile powder at Mexican markets (where it might be labeled "pasilla chile powder"), at some supermarkets, and spice shops. If you can find good-quality spiced nuts at the store, you can make the salad with those and save a bit of time.

Wild Rice

¾ cup wild rice

Salt

Dressing

3 tablespoons extra-virgin olive oil

2 generous tablespoons finely chopped shallot

1 tablespoon apple cider vinegar

½ teaspoon grated orange zest

2 tablespoons orange juice

1 teaspoon honey

¼ teaspoon salt

Salad

8 ounces Brussels sprouts, trimmed and halved

1 tablespoon extra-virgin olive oil

¼ cup chopped pitted Deglet Noor or other dates

½ cup Ancho-Spiced Pecans (page 219)

2 ounces soft fresh goat cheese, crumbled (optional)

2 tablespoons fresh Italian parsley leaves (optional)

For the wild rice: Boil the wild rice in a medium saucepan of salted water until very tender, about 45 minutes. Drain the rice well and transfer to a medium bowl. Cool completely. *(The rice can be prepared up to 2 days ahead. Cover and refrigerate.)*

For the dressing: In a jar, whisk or shake the oil, shallot, vinegar, orange zest and juice, honey, and salt to blend. *(The dressing can be prepared up to 2 days ahead. Cover the jar and refrigerate.)*

For the salad: Preheat the oven to 450°F.

Toss the Brussels sprouts on heavy small sheet pan with the oil. Sprinkle with salt and roast until browned and tender, about 10 minutes. Cool.

Add the Brussels sprouts and dates to the wild rice. Add the dressing and toss well. Sprinkle with the pecans. Top with the goat cheese and parsley, if desired, and serve.

brown rice grape leaf salad

4 SERVINGS / GF

A favorite from my book *Salad for Dinner*, this deconstructed dolma dish is a winner. I reintroduce it to you because making it one day, I realized I'd run out of jarred brined grape leaves. With relief I remembered the robust grapevine winding about my garden. Simmered briefly in salted water, cooled, and chopped, the leaves of the vine were just right, and the time it took to prepare them was much shorter than a trip to my favorite Middle Eastern market.

1 cup uncooked brown rice, rinsed, or 1 (10-ounce) package frozen cooked brown rice

½ teaspoon salt

5 tablespoons extra-virgin olive oil

3 tablespoons fresh lemon juice

12 fresh grape leaves, or ⅓ cup finely chopped rinsed and drained brined grape leaves

½ cup currants

½ cup toasted pine nuts or roasted shelled pistachios

¼ cup thinly sliced green onions

½ cup crumbled feta cheese (about 1½ ounces)

2 tablespoons minced fresh cilantro

2 tablespoons minced fresh dill

2 tablespoons minced fresh mint

6 cups arugula or mixed greens

Plain Greek yogurt (optional)

Lemon wedges

If using uncooked rice: Bring 2 cups water to a boil in a heavy medium saucepan. Add the rice and salt. Return the water to a boil, then reduce the heat to very low. Cover and simmer until the rice is tender and the water has been absorbed, about 40 minutes. Remove from the heat and let stand, covered, for 5 minutes. Transfer the rice to a bowl, stir in 1 tablespoon of the oil and 1 tablespoon of the lemon juice, and let cool to room temperature.

If using packaged frozen rice: Place the rice in a large microwave-safe bowl. Add 1 tablespoon water. Cover and microwave on high for 1 minute, or until the rice softens. Mix in 1 tablespoon of the oil and 1 tablespoon lemon juice.

Bring 3 inches of salted water to a simmer in a heavy medium saucepan. Working in batches, add half the grape leaves and simmer until olive green in color, about 30 seconds. Using tongs, carefully transfer to a plate to drain; repeat with the remaining grape leaves. Cool.

Chop the grape leaves and stir them into the cooled rice along with the currants, nuts, green onions, cheese, cilantro, dill, and mint. Mix in 2 tablespoons of the oil and 1 tablespoon of the lemon juice.

In a separate large bowl, toss the arugula with the remaining 2 tablespoons oil and 1 tablespoon lemon juice. Season the greens with salt. Divide the greens among plates and top with the rice salad. Spoon a dollop of yogurt alongside the salad, if desired. Garnish with lemon wedges and serve.

mushrooms, barley, dandelion greens

4 TO 6 SERVINGS

You can make this warm salad with any kind of mushrooms. My go-to is a blend of shiitake, cremini, and oyster mushrooms. To prep the shiitakes, I cut away the tough stem and slice the cap, and for the oyster mushrooms, I just tear them into ¾-inch fan-shaped pieces. I love the counterbalance of creamy mushrooms with bitter greens, but if dandelion greens make you grimace, use spinach.

¾ cup pearled barley

3 cups water

½ teaspoon salt, plus more to taste

6 tablespoons extra-virgin olive oil

1¼ pounds mushrooms, such as oyster, cremini, shiitake, and button, sliced or torn (about 8 cups)

1 tablespoon butter

1 large shallot, finely chopped

4 garlic cloves, finely chopped

2 teaspoons chopped fresh thyme, or ½ teaspoon dried

6 cups dandelion greens (about 2 bunches), torn into 2- to 3-inch pieces

3 tablespoons sherry vinegar

½ cup grated Parmesan cheese, plus more for sprinkling

Freshly ground black pepper

⅓ cup sherry

⅓ cup heavy cream

Combine the barley, water, and salt in a heavy medium saucepan and bring to a boil. Reduce the heat to medium-low and simmer until the barley is tender and the liquid has been absorbed, about 40 minutes. Transfer the barley to a bowl and toss with 1 tablespoon of the oil. *(The barley can be cooked up to 3 days ahead; cover and refrigerate. Bring to room temperature before continuing.)*

Heat 2 tablespoons of the remaining oil in a heavy, very large skillet over medium-high heat. Add the mushrooms and sauté until they release some moisture and begin to become browned and tender, about 10 minutes. Using a wooden spoon, push the mushrooms to the edge of the pan. Add the butter to the center of the pan along with the shallot, garlic, and thyme and sauté the shallot mixture until it begins to become tender, about 3 minutes. Stir in the mushrooms, sprinkle with salt, and sauté until the mushrooms are tender, about 10 minutes. *(The mushrooms can be prepared ahead up to this point. Cover loosely and let stand at room temperature for up to 2 hours. Reheat over medium-high heat before continuing.)*

Meanwhile, combine the dandelion greens, barley, remaining 3 tablespoons oil, the vinegar, and the cheese in a large bowl and toss well. Season with salt and pepper. Divide the barley mixture among plates.

Stir the sherry and cream into the mushrooms and simmer until the pan is deglazed and the mushrooms are coated, about 1 minute. Season with salt and pepper. Top the barley mixture with the mushrooms, sprinkle with cheese, and serve.

charred green beans and parsnips, farro, radicchio, gorgonzola, walnuts

4 SERVINGS

Parsnips are the starchy white cousins of carrots. When roasted, they take on a satisfying chewy texture. Mixing the thinly sliced shallots into the hot-from-the-oven green beans softens and sweetens them. Enjoy this wintery salad with a glass of Barbera d'Asti.

1 cup farro

Salt

1 pound green beans, trimmed

4 tablespoons extra-virgin olive oil

1 pound parsnips, trimmed and sliced into ¼-inch-thick rounds

Salt and freshly ground black pepper

1 small shallot, thinly sliced

1 small head radicchio, sliced

Best-quality balsamic vinegar (about 3 tablespoons)

Best-quality extra-virgin olive oil, for finishing (about 2 tablespoons; optional)

½ cup crumbled Gorgonzola cheese (about 2 ounces)

½ cup chopped walnuts or hazelnuts, toasted

Cook the farro in rapidly boiling salted water until tender, about 25 minutes. Drain the farro well. *(The farro can be cooked up to 3 days ahead; cover and refrigerate.)*

Preheat the oven to 425°F.

Toss the green beans with 1 tablespoon of the olive oil on a heavy large sheet pan and spread them out into a single layer. Toss the parsnips with 1 tablespoon of the remaining olive oil on a separate heavy large sheet pan and spread them out into a single layer. Sprinkle with salt and pepper and roast, stirring once or twice, until charred in places and tender, about 15 minutes. Remove from the oven, immediately add the farro and shallot to the green beans on the pan, and toss well. Transfer the green bean mixture and parsnips to a shallow bowl and mix in the radicchio. Drizzle with vinegar and the remaining 2 tablespoons olive oil. Finish with best-quality olive oil, if desired. Crumble over the cheese, sprinkle with the nuts, and serve.

arroz con cosas (paella-style salad)

6 TO 8 SERVINGS / GF, VEGAN

This delicious saffron-infused rice salad is based on paella, the Valencian classic. *Arroz con cosas*, or "rice with things," is the name given to saffron and rice dishes that fall short of being authentic. The "things" in this salad are abundant in spring and early summer, but feel free to adapt the recipe to any season—roasted peppers, grilled zucchini, and chickpeas in late summer; marinated mushrooms, cauliflower, and Brussels sprouts in fall.

Cosas

1 tablespoon extra-virgin olive oil

8 ounces romano (flat green) beans, trimmed and cut into 2-inch pieces

1½ cups fresh or frozen double-shelled fava beans or frozen shelled edamame

1½ cups frozen peas

1 bunch asparagus, trimmed, cut into 2-inch pieces

Salt

½ cup water

10 to 12 ounces grilled or marinated artichoke hearts or quarters, drained

8 ounces cherry tomatoes, cut in half

8 ounces mini bell peppers, trimmed and sliced, or 1 large red bell pepper, diced

1 cup pimiento-stuffed Spanish olives, sliced

6 green onions, sliced

½ cup chopped fresh Italian parsley

Rice

3½ cups water

2 garlic cloves, chopped

½ teaspoon saffron threads

½ teaspoon salt

1 pound long-grain white rice (about 2⅓ cups)

Extra-virgin olive oil

Dressing

½ cup extra-virgin olive oil

⅓ cup sherry vinegar

1 tablespoon minced fresh oregano

1 large garlic clove, finely grated or crushed with a garlic press

1 teaspoon smoked paprika

¾ teaspoon salt

For the cosas: Heat the oil in a heavy, very large skillet over medium-high heat. Add the romano beans and toss to coat. Add the peas, favas, and asparagus and sprinkle with salt. Add the water, bring to a simmer, and cook until the water evaporates and the vegetables are crisp-tender, about 4 minutes. Transfer to a large bowl and cool completely.

Add the artichoke hearts, tomatoes, bell peppers, olives, green onions, and parsley. *(The cosas can be prepared up to 1 day ahead; cover and refrigerate.)*

For the rice: Bring the water, garlic, saffron, and salt to a boil in a heavy large saucepan over high heat. Add the rice, reduce the heat to low, cover, and simmer until the rice is tender and the liquid has been absorbed, about 15 minutes. Brush a large sheet pan with oil. Spread the rice out in a single layer on the pan and cool completely.

Meanwhile, whisk ingredients for dressing to blend in a small bowl. Add the rice to the cosas, toss with dressing to taste, and serve.

pulse salads

Beans, lentils, and peas are pulses. A pulse is technically a seed—think "Jack and the Beanstalk"—and like they are in the fairy tale, pulses are pretty magical. Inexpensive and loaded with protein, fiber, vitamins, and minerals, pulses are a personal favorite. Soaked and simmered, boiled or dumped from a can, pulses can be transformed into an elegant or homespun salad suitable for a dinner party or a kitchen supper. Indeed, canned beans are so versatile that they are a featured addition to salads in most sections of this book. Chickpeas, aka garbanzo beans, are a powerhouse: they add protein, vitamins, minerals, and fiber to a number of recipes in this book. I even include in this chapter a Falafel-ette salad, which features quick-to-make mini falafels, to highlight the versatility of the chickpea in flour form.

Lentils are another ingredient prominently featured in this chapter but also scattered throughout the book. Lentils are packed with protein and iron—sought-after nutrients for a plant-forward diet—but beyond being so good for you, they are simply just so good.

White beans, very large as with the corona bean or quick and creamy as with canned cannellini beans, are also featured. Often overlooked mung beans make for a great salad, and green peas add sweetness, plant protein, vitamins, and minerals to an India-inspired potato salad.

corona bean salad

4 TO 6 SERVINGS / GF

My mother made three-bean salad for picnics when I was a child. I loved how the tart vinaigrette made the tomatoes, onions, and beans so sweet by contrast. Here's a fresher version of that favorite that needs only two beans—because the beans are colossal. Corona beans are enormous runner beans. With their creamy interior and sturdy exterior, they make an excellent salad bean. Also, their huge size and cute shape make them a whole lotta fun to eat. I order my Royal Coronas from Rancho Gordo Beans. If you can't get your hands on a package, you can substitute one 14.5-ounce can of red kidney beans and one 14- to 16-ounce can of chickpeas, rinsed and drained, just like Mom did. Round out the meal with a fresh goat cheese and a crusty loaf of country bread.

Corona Beans

12 ounces dried corona beans, soaked overnight

1 small yellow onion, cut in half

3 bay leaves, preferably fresh

1 dried arbol chile

3 tablespoons red wine vinegar

2 tablespoons extra-virgin olive oil

1 teaspoon salt

Salad

1 pound green beans, trimmed and cut in half

Salt

1¼ pounds best-quality tomatoes, cut into wedges

1 red onion, halved and thinly sliced

Oregano Vinaigrette (page 54)

Salt and freshly cracked black pepper

4 ounces (or more) soft fresh goat cheese

For the beans: Drain the beans and place in a large pot. Cover the beans with 2 to 3 inches of fresh water and add the onion, bay leaves, and chile. Bring the beans to a simmer over medium-high heat, then reduce the heat to medium-low and simmer until just beginning to become tender, adding more water if necessary, about 1½ hours. Add the vinegar, oil, and salt and simmer until the beans are tender yet retain their shape, adding more water if necessary, about 30 minutes. Cool the beans in the cooking liquid. *(The beans can be cooked up to 4 days ahead. Store covered in their liquid in the refrigerator.)*

For the salad: Cook the green beans in a saucepan of rapidly boiling salted water until crisp-tender, about 3 minutes. Drain and cool in cold water. Drain well. Drain the corona beans and place in a large bowl with the green beans. Add the tomatoes and red onion. Gently mix in the vinaigrette and season with salt and pepper. Crumble the goat cheese over the salad and serve.

french lentils, roasted beets, dried cherries, rosemary, goat cheese

4 SERVINGS / GF

Vegetarians tend to eat lots of lentils. Even if you love lentils like I do, some preparations taste dull and uninspired. This salad excites the palate with the unexpected additions of cherries and rosemary. If you want this salad to come together extra quick, you can use a 17.6-ounce package of vacuum-sealed steamed lentils and two 8-ounce packages of vacuum-sealed steamed beets.

Beets

1 pound medium beets (about 4)

Extra-virgin olive oil or vegetable oil

Lentils

1 cup dried French or black lentils

Salad

4 celery stalks, diced

1 shallot, finely chopped (about ½ cup)

½ cup coarsely chopped fresh Italian parsley

¼ cup chopped dried sour cherries

⅓ cup extra-virgin olive oil

2 tablespoons balsamic vinegar

1 tablespoon red wine vinegar

1 teaspoon chopped fresh rosemary

½ teaspoon salt, plus more to taste

Freshly cracked black pepper

4 cups mixed greens

6 to 8 ounces soft fresh goat cheese, crumbled

For the beets: Preheat the oven to 375°F.

Arrange the beets in the center of a sheet of foil. Drizzle the beets with a small amount of oil and enclose in the foil. Roast the beets until tender, about 1 hour. Cool. *(The beets can be prepared up to 3 days ahead; refrigerate.)* Peel and quarter the beets.

For the lentils: Cook the lentils in a saucepan of rapidly boiling salted water until tender, about 20 minutes. Drain well and cool completely.

For the salad: Combine the lentils, celery, shallot, parsley, and cherries in a large bowl. Whisk together the oil, both vinegars, the rosemary, and salt to blend in a small bowl for the dressing. Pour the dressing over the lentil mixture and toss to coat. Season with salt and pepper. *(The lentils can be prepared ahead. Cover and refrigerate for up to 2 days.)*

Add the greens to the lentils and toss well. Serve topped with the crumbled goat cheese.

muhammara, turnip, pomegranate, and dandelion green slaw, walnuts

4 SERVINGS / VEGAN OPTION

Muhammara is a deeply flavored red pepper and walnut dip. The muhammara in Reem Kassis's book *The Palestinian Table* is my favorite. Her book is an excellent resource on Arabic cuisine, in particular the food and culture of Palestine—and it's a pleasure to both read and cook from. I've adapted her muhammara to pair with a garden–inspired slaw. Baby turnips are so tender, they don't require peeling. Look for them at farmers', specialty, or Japanese markets. If you can't find them, a peeled mature turnip will do just fine.

Muhammara Dip

1 generous cup drained jarred roasted red peppers (about one 12-ounce jar)

¼ cup extra-virgin olive oil

¼ cup pomegranate molasses

1 tablespoon tahini

1 teaspoon Aleppo pepper or ancho chile powder

1 teaspoon paprika

¼ teaspoon ground cumin

½ teaspoon salt

1 cup walnuts, toasted

¼ cup breadcrumbs, preferably homemade

1 tablespoon honey or agave nectar

Slaw

2 tablespoons fresh lemon juice

2 tablespoons extra-virgin olive oil

¼ teaspoon salt

4 cups mixed greens, such as thinly sliced dandelion greens, baby kale leaves, and wild arugula

1 bunch baby turnips, trimmed, halved, and sliced, or 1 large mature turnip, peeled and cut into matchstick-sized pieces

1 cup cooked or purchased vacuum-sealed steamed lentils

Finishing

½ cup pomegranate seeds

½ cup walnuts, toasted

⅓ cup fresh mint leaves

For the dip: Combine the peppers, oil, molasses, tahini, Aleppo pepper or chile powder, paprika, cumin, and salt in the bowl of a food processor and process until smooth. Add the walnuts and breadcrumbs and process until the walnuts are finely chopped. Season with honey and additional salt. *(The dip can be prepared 4 days ahead. Transfer to a jar and keep refrigerated.)*

For the slaw: Whisk together the lemon juice, oil, and salt in a large bowl. Add the greens, turnips, and lentils and toss to coat with the lemon juice mixture.

Spoon and spread the dip over plates and top with the slaw. Sprinkle the salads with the pomegranate seeds, walnuts, and mint leaves and serve.

falafel-ette salad

4 TO 6 SERVINGS / GF

Inspired by Israeli falafel sandwiches, this salad features the works—smashed cucumbers, creamy cabbage, tender eggplant, tomatoes, lettuce, tangy tahini sauce, and crispy bits of fried herbed falafel. The "falafel-ettes" come together easily with chickpea (garbanzo bean) flour. Look for chickpea flour at health food stores and in the gluten-free section of the supermarket; Bob's Red Mill is a very good brand.

Cabbage Salad

4 cups thinly sliced red cabbage

2 tablespoons vinegar (white, red wine, or apple cider)

½ teaspoon salt

⅓ cup labneh, plain Greek yogurt, or sour cream

¼ cup chopped fresh Italian parsley, mint, cilantro, and/or dill

Eggplant

1½ pounds eggplant (about 2 medium globe or 4 long, thin eggplants), cut into ¾-inch chunks

1 scant teaspoon salt

Falafel-ettes

1 cup yellow onion chunks (about ½ large)

1 cup packed fresh Italian parsley, mint, and/or dill sprigs

1 cup packed fresh cilantro sprigs

1 large jalapeño chile, stemmed

3 large garlic cloves, peeled

1 tablespoon extra-virgin olive oil

1 cup chickpea (garbanzo bean) flour

1 tablespoon ground coriander

1 tablespoon ground cumin

1 teaspoon salt

½ teaspoon baking soda

The Rest

Extra-virgin olive oil for frying

Aleppo pepper

Lettuce leaves

1½ cups cherry tomatoes, cut in half

Smashed Cucumbers with Mint (page 148)

Tahini Sauce (recipe follows)

Harrissa, homemade (page 213) or purchased, thinned with water to a drizzling consistency

For the cabbage salad: Combine the cabbage, vinegar, and salt in a medium bowl and toss to combine. With the back of a spoon, press the cabbage firmly a few times until it softens slightly. Mix in the labneh and herbs. *(The cabbage can be prepared up to 2 days ahead. Cover and refrigerate.)*

For the eggplant: Toss the eggplant with the salt in a colander set over the sink or a bowl and let stand for at least an hour or two (or up to 8 hours, covered, at cool room temperature).

recipe continues

For the falafel-ettes: Combine the onion, herbs, chile, garlic, and oil in a food processor. Using on/off turns, pulse until the mixture is very finely chopped. Add the chickpea flour and sprinkle in the coriander, cumin, salt, and baking soda. Process the mixture until blended. Transfer to a small bowl. *(The falafel mixture can be prepared up to 8 hours ahead. Cover and keep at cool room temperature.)*

For frying: Heat ½ inch of oil in heavy large skillet over medium-high heat. Working in batches and adding more oil as necessary, drop the falafel mixture by marble-sized spoonfuls into the hot oil and fry until browned, about 2 minutes. Transfer to a plate and keep warm.

If there is quite a bit of oil remaining in the pan, pour off all but a thin layer. Add the eggplant and cook until tender, about 4 minutes. Season with Aleppo pepper.

Line a platter or plates with lettuce. Mound the cabbage, cucumbers, eggplant, tomatoes, and falafel-ettes atop the lettuce. Drizzle with tahini sauce, dollop with harissa, and serve.

tahini sauce

MAKES 1 GENEROUS CUP

Most people first meet tahini sauce at the falafel shop. Made with just three ingredients, if you don't count water and salt, it stirs together magically to form a creamy, tart, and tangy sauce that's delicious on cooked and raw vegetables, pulses and greens, salads and fritters.

½ cup tahini

⅓ cup fresh lemon juice

¼ cup water

2 garlic cloves, finely grated or crushed with a garlic press

1 teaspoon salt

In a medium bowl, whisk the ingredients to blend. *(The tahini sauce can be prepared up to 1 week ahead. Transfer to a jar, cover, and refrigerate.)*

beet hummus, fioretto, pine nut gremolata

4 SERVINGS / GF, VEGAN

The first time I saw Fioretto at the farmers' market, I thought the farmer had let the cauliflower go to seed and wondered why the freaky-looking vegetable was selling out fast. Fioretto, or flowering cauliflower, looks like a loose head of cauliflower with thin, pale green stalks and flowery tips reaching randomly through. Fioretto isn't a mutant; it's a hybrid of cauliflower and broccoli. It is mild, slightly sweet, and delicious both cooked and raw. When grown in warmer climates, the florets can have a slight pale pink hue. While Fioretto is a farmers' market favorite, it's just beginning to become available at better supermarkets. If you can't find it, Broccolini is good in this salad too.

Hummus

8 ounces beets
(2 or 3 medium)

1 (14- to 16-ounce) can chickpeas, rinsed and drained

4 to 5 tablespoons fresh lemon juice

2 tablespoons tahini

2 tablespoons extra-virgin olive oil

2 garlic cloves, peeled

¾ teaspoon salt

1 ice cube

Fioretto

1 head Fioretto
(flowering cauliflower)

3 tablespoons extra-virgin olive oil

1 tablespoon fresh lemon juice

Salt

½ cup water

Gremolata

¼ cup pine nuts

1 green onion, very thinly sliced

2 tablespoons extra-virgin olive oil

1 tablespoon finely chopped fresh cilantro

1 tablespoon finely chopped fresh dill

1 garlic clove, finely grated or crushed with a garlic press

1 scant teaspoon lime or lemon zest

For the hummus: Trim, peel, and thickly slice the beets. Cover the beets with 2 inches of water in a heavy small saucepan. Bring to a simmer and cook until the beets are very tender when pierced with a knife, about 30 minutes. Remove from the heat and cool.

Drain the beets and put them in a food processor with the chickpeas, 4 tablespoons of the lemon juice, the tahini, oil, garlic, and salt. Process until a smooth mixture begins to form. Add the ice cube and process until the hummus is very smooth. Taste and add additional lemon juice, if desired. *(The hummus can be prepared up to 4 days ahead. Transfer to a bowl, cover, and refrigerate.)*

recipe continues

For the Fioretto: Trim off the delicate branching florets from the Fioretto head. In a medium bowl, toss the branching florets with 2 tablespoons of the oil, the lemon juice, and a generous pinch of salt and set aside. Cut the head into 1- to 2-inch florets. Heat the remaining 1 tablespoon oil in a heavy large saucepan over medium-high heat. Add the florets and cook, undisturbed, until they begin to sizzle, about 1 minute. Stir in the water and sprinkle with salt. Reduce the heat to medium, cover, and cook until the water evaporates and the florets are just tender, about 4 minutes. Uncover and cool completely.

For the gremolata: Toast the pine nuts in a heavy small skillet over medium heat, stirring, until they just turn golden brown, about 1 minute. Transfer to a small bowl and cool completely. Stir in the green onion, oil, cilantro, dill, garlic, and lime zest.

When ready to serve: Spoon the hummus onto plates. Top the hummus with the cooked and raw Fioretto, dividing it evenly. Spoon the gremolata over the Fioretto and serve.

GREMOLATA

Gremolata is an Italian condiment. Unlike most toppings that get spooned or drizzled, gremolata is intended for sprinkling. Traditional gremolata is simply a combination of minced parsley, lemon zest, and garlic. The bright zestiness of the topping adds zip and cuts through rich foods. Classically, it's used as a fresh, herbal punch atop unctuous, slow-braised osso buco. For me, any combo of fresh herb, garlic, and citrus qualifies as gremolata, even if I add a little oil or a few nuts to it. I use it as an herb-based flavor enhancer for any rich or creamy food and I season it accordingly. Orange, grapefruit, kumquat, and lime zest can play with herbs beyond parsley. The pine nut, lime, dill, and cilantro version that I use to finish the Fioretto salad offers a clean contrast to the creamy, smooth, and earthy-tasting beet hummus.

hummus msabaha, curly endive, zhoug

2 SERVINGS / GF, VEGAN

Msabaha is a whole bean hummus that's popular in the Middle East. If you have the zhoug and tahini sauce on hand, this comes together in a flash, which is satisfying after a busy day. If you don't have curly endive, use another flavorful green. Zhoug is spicy green relish from Yemen. If you don't have the time or desire to make it, you can substitute purchased zhoug, or simply add a handful of chopped parsley and an extra squeeze of lemon to the endive instead.

1 (14- to 16-ounce) can chickpeas, rinsed and drained

3 tablespoons Zhoug (page 214)

1 tablespoon fresh lemon juice

2 tablespoons extra-virgin olive oil

6 cups bite-sized pieces curly endive (about 1 head)

Tahini Sauce (page 96)

Aleppo pepper

Pat the chickpeas dry with a clean dish towel and set aside.

Whisk together the zhoug, lemon juice, and 1 tablespoon of the oil in a large bowl. Add the endive and toss well.

Heat the remaining 1 tablespoon oil in a heavy medium saucepan over medium-high heat. Add the chickpeas and cook until they begin to become golden brown, about 2 minutes. Add the tahini sauce and stir until the chickpeas thicken slightly and some incorporate into the sauce, about 2 minutes.

Divide the greens between two plates, top with the msabaha, sprinkle with Aleppo pepper, and serve.

black lentil, roast cauliflower, red cabbage slaw, piri-piri sauce

SERVES 4 TO 6 / GF, VEGAN

I heard about delicious piri-piri sauce from my daughter Theresa, who enjoyed the spicy condiment when she was working as a cellar intern in South Africa. Made with red chiles, herbs, and tart vinegar and aromatics, the hot sauce has roots in Portugal and Southern African countries. Piri-piri adds verve to this colorful mix of lentils, cabbage, and roasted cauliflower. Sale-priced golden berries, aka cape gooseberries, were an impulse buy that proved to be an inspired addition to this mix.

1 large cauliflower, cut into ½- to 1-inch florets

½ cup plus 2 tablespoons extra-virgin olive oil

1 tablespoon Piri-Piri Sauce (page 213), plus more for serving

Salt

1 cup dried black or French green lentils

1 bay leaf, preferably fresh

3 cups chopped red cabbage (about ¼ head)

6 ounces golden berries (cape gooseberries; about 1 cup), or sweet cherry tomatoes, cut in half

½ cup minced sweet onion

¼ cup chopped fresh cilantro

3 tablespoons red wine vinegar

1 cup chopped roasted peanuts

Preheat the oven to 425°F.

Toss the cauliflower with 2 tablespoons of the oil and the piri-piri sauce on a heavy large sheet pan. Sprinkle lightly with salt and roast, stirring once or twice, until tender and well browned, about 25 minutes. Cool and transfer to a large bowl.

Meanwhile, cover the lentils and bay leaf with a few inches of water in a heavy small saucepan. Add a generous pinch of salt and bring to a boil over medium-high heat. Lower the heat and simmer until the lentils are just tender, about 20 minutes. Drain well and cool completely.

Add the lentils, cabbage, golden berries, onion, cilantro, remaining ½ cup oil, and the vinegar to the cauliflower and toss well. *(The dish can be prepared up to 1 day ahead. Cover and refrigerate.)*

Just before serving, stir in the peanuts. Serve the slaw with a generous drizzle of piri-piri sauce.

black beans, brown rice, scorched kale

4 SERVINGS / GF

The combo of beans and rice is a beloved staple all over Latin America. The humble blend results in a complete protein, meaning it contains a balance of all nine essential amino acids. Scorching kale over or under a flame both tenderizes the leaves and adds deep, smoky flavor. You can do the torching over a barbecue grill or stovetop burner, or under the broiler. Cotija cheese is a crumbly hard Mexican cheese; it's perfectly salted for this salad, but feta also makes a fine option.

2 cups freshly cooked brown rice, or 1 (10-ounce) bag frozen cooked brown rice, prepared according to the package directions

1 (15-ounce) can black beans, rinsed and drained

1 small bunch radishes, trimmed and sliced into rounds

2 green onions, trimmed and sliced

¼ cup chopped fresh cilantro

1 to 2 tablespoons minced seeded jalapeño chile

¼ cup fresh lime juice

¼ cup extra-virgin olive oil

2 teaspoons ground cumin

½ teaspoon salt

12 kale leaves

2 avocados, sliced

3 ounces crumbled Cotija or feta cheese (about ½ cup)

½ cup toasted pepitas (green pumpkin seeds), for garnish

2 limes, cut into wedges

In a large bowl, combine the rice, beans, radishes, green onions, cilantro, and jalapeño. Whisk together the lime juice, oil, cumin, and salt in a small bowl to blend for the dressing. Drizzle ¼ cup of the dressing over the rice mixture and stir to combine. Set aside.

To char the kale using a gas burner: Using tongs, hold each kale leaf by the stem over an open gas flame set on high, turning until toasted and lightly charred at the edges, about 1 minute per leaf.

To char the kale on a grill: Heat a grill to medium. Lightly brush the grates with oil. Arrange the kale in a single layer on the grill and cook, turning once or twice, until just toasted and lightly charred at the edges, about 1 minute per leaf.

To char the kale under the broiler: Arrange the leaves in a single layer on a heavy large sheet pan and char lightly on both sides. Cool slightly, then coarsely chop. Mix the kale into the salad. *(The salad can be prepared up to 1 day ahead. Cover and refrigerate the salad and the extra dressing separately.)*

Divide the salad among bowls and top with the avocado slices. Sprinkle with the cheese and pepitas. Drizzle the remaining dressing over the salads, garnish with the lime wedges, and serve.

white bean, broiled treviso, fig, olive

2 SERVINGS / GF, VEGAN

Treviso, like radicchio, is a burgundy-hued chicory. Treviso grows into elongated heads that are sweeter and a bit looser than radicchio. It stores well in the crisper so it can quickly and conveniently star in this surprisingly fancy-tasting pantry dinner.

¼ cup extra-virgin olive oil, plus more for brushing

3 tablespoons red wine vinegar

1 garlic clove, finely grated or crushed with a garlic press

¼ teaspoon salt, plus more to taste

1 (14- to 16-ounce) can cannellini beans, rinsed and drained

⅓ cup diced dried Mission figs (about 7)

¼ medium red onion, halved and thinly sliced

8 oil-cured black olives, pitted and very coarsely chopped

2 tablespoons fresh Italian parsley leaves

1 head Treviso, cut in half lengthwise

Freshly ground black pepper

Fancy balsamic vinegar, for drizzling (optional)

Stir together the oil, red wine vinegar, garlic, and salt to blend in a shallow baking dish that's large enough to accommodate the Treviso. Add the beans, figs, onion, olives, and parsley and stir to coat. Let the mixture marinate at room temperature for 1 to 3 hours.

Preheat the broiler.

Place the Treviso, cut-side up, atop the beans. Brush the Treviso lightly with oil and season lightly with salt and pepper. Broil until the Treviso is just browned and the beans are warmed. Transfer the Treviso and beans to plates, drizzle with balsamic vinegar, if desired, and serve.

potato, pea, mango, yogurt, spice, spinach

4 SERVINGS / GF

This curried salad has it all—tender potatoes and peas, crunchy cucumber and onion, sweet mango, piquant jalapeño, fresh greens and herbs, all napped with a delicate curry cream. This salad can be made ahead.

Dressing

1 rounded teaspoon coriander seeds

1 scant teaspoon cumin seeds

⅓ cup plain whole-milk yogurt

⅓ cup sour cream or labneh

1 teaspoon ground turmeric

1 garlic clove, finely grated or crushed with a garlic press

½ teaspoon salt

Salad

1 pound peewee potatoes, cut in half

1½ cups frozen peas

½ hothouse cucumber, quartered lengthwise and sliced

½ cup chopped red onion

1 jalapeño chile, seeded and finely diced

¼ cup fresh cilantro leaves, plus more for garnish

1 ripe mango, peeled, pitted, and diced

4 cups baby spinach leaves and/or bite-sized pieces red mustard greens (optional)

Fresh cilantro leaves

Nigella seeds (optional)

For the dressing: Toast the coriander and cumin seeds in a heavy small skillet over medium-high heat until fragrant, about 1 minute. Cool slightly and coarsely grind with a mortar and pestle or in a spice grinder. Combine the toasted spices with the yogurt, sour cream, turmeric, garlic, and salt in a large bowl.

For the salad: Boil the potatoes in a large saucepan of salted water until just tender, about 8 minutes. Remove the pan from the heat; add the frozen peas and let stand for 2 minutes. Drain well and cool completely.

Add the potatoes and peas to the dressing along with the cucumber, onion, chile, and cilantro. *(The salad can be prepared up to 3 days ahead. Cover and refrigerate.)*

Add the mango to the salad. Line plates with spinach and/or mustard greens, if desired. Spoon the salad atop the greens and garnish with cilantro. Sprinkle with nigella seeds, if desired, and serve.

grilled broccoli, mushrooms, peppers, white bean puree, chimichurri

4 TO 6 SERVINGS / GF, VEGAN

This salad is inspired by the parillada of Argentina. If you have been to Buenos Aires or are familiar with that meaty meal, you might be laughing. But grilled, broccoli, portobellos, and peppers develop umami, and the white bean puree is unctuous and smoky. Sauced with chimichurri, Argentina's famous vinegary condiment, the resulting salad is rich and savory with no passport or butcher required.

White Bean Puree

2 (15- to 16-ounce) cans cannellini beans, rinsed and drained

½ cup extra-virgin olive oil

2 garlic cloves, peeled

1 teaspoon smoked paprika

Salt and freshly ground black pepper

Chimichurri

¼ cup finely chopped shallot

1 bay leaf, preferably fresh, torn into 4 pieces

6 tablespoons extra-virgin olive oil

4 garlic cloves, minced

½ teaspoon red pepper flakes

3 tablespoons red wine vinegar

¼ cup finely chopped fresh Italian parsley

1 teaspoon minced fresh thyme

Salt and freshly ground black pepper

Salad

1 large bunch broccoli, 1¼ to 1½ pounds

12 ounces portobello mushrooms, cut crosswise into ½-inch-thick slices

2 red bell peppers, cut into 1-inch-wide strips

Extra-virgin olive oil, for brushing

For the white bean puree: Combine the beans, oil, garlic, and smoked paprika in a food processor and process, stopping to scrape down the sides as necessary, until smooth. Season with salt and black pepper. *(The puree can be prepared ahead. Cover and refrigerate for up to 3 days.)*

For the chimichurri: Combine the shallot and bay leaf in a small bowl. Heat the oil in a heavy small skillet over medium heat. Add the garlic and red pepper flakes and swirl gently until the garlic is tender, about 1 minute (do not brown the garlic). Remove from the heat and stir in the shallot mixture. Add the vinegar and let stand until cool. Stir in the parsley and thyme. Season generously with salt and black pepper.

For the salad: Heat a grill to medium. Cut the broccoli into long-stemmed florets, ¾ to 1 inch thick. Brush the broccoli, mushrooms, and bell pepper strips with oil and grill until well browned on both sides and tender, about 12 minutes for the broccoli and mushrooms and 8 minutes for the bell peppers.

Spoon the puree onto plates or a platter and top with the broccoli mixture. Drizzle the chimichurri over the salads, and serve.

mung beans, caramelized onions, sun-dried tomatoes

4 SERVINGS / GF, VEGAN

Credit goes to Bulgarian-Turkish-English chef Silvena Rowe for this simple yet deeply satisfying dish. Her cookbooks are full of colorful ingredients combined in inspired and attractive ways. Her salad of tender mung beans and dulcet caramelized onions demands flattering imitation. In my rendition I swap her shallots and mustard for olives and garlic for a different yet similar salty-sharp bite. If you're not acquainted with the small green pulse, it's a good bean to know, as they taste great, cook quickly, and have a pleasant tender-pop texture.

1 cup (8 ounces) dried mung beans, soaked in cold water overnight and drained

½ teaspoon salt, plus more to taste

¼ cup plus 2 tablespoons extra-virgin olive oil

3 large yellow onions, sliced (about 6 cups)

½ cup drained olive oil–packed sun-dried tomatoes, sliced

½ cup fresh Italian parsley leaves

3 tablespoons red wine vinegar

1 garlic clove, finely grated or crushed with a garlic press

½ cup pitted kalamata olives, chopped (optional)

Freshly ground black and Aleppo pepper

2 (or more) teaspoons nigella seeds (optional)

Bring the mung beans and enough cool water to cover by a few inches to a boil in a heavy large saucepan. Reduce the heat to medium-low and simmer until the beans begin to become tender, about 10 minutes. Add a generous pinch of salt and simmer until the beans are very tender but retain their shape, about 10 minutes longer. Drain, transfer to a large bowl, and cool completely.

Meanwhile, heat ¼ cup of the oil in a heavy large skillet over medium heat. Add the onions, sprinkle with salt, and cook, stirring often, until caramelized, about 40 minutes. Cool completely, then add to the mung beans. *(The onions and mung beans can be prepared up to 1 day ahead. Cover and refrigerate.)*

Add the sun-dried tomatoes and parsley to the salad. Whisk together the remaining 2 tablespoons oil, the vinegar, garlic, and salt to blend in a small bowl and add to the salad. Add the olives, if desired, and season with additional salt, black pepper, and Aleppo pepper. Serve sprinkled with the nigella seeds, if desired.

salads
with seeds

This chapter began as a collection of quinoa salads. Quinoa is an indispensable ingredient for plant-forward recipes. Pseudograins, or pseudocereals, are processed and used in similar ways as grains but are in fact seeds. Quinoa, the seed of an amaranth variety, is rich in protein, fiber, vitamins, and minerals. A neutral and highly adaptable flavor and quick cooking time make quinoa a salad go-to. Quinoa is available at most grocery stores in white, red, black, or tricolor options. White is the mildest tasting, red is a little nuttier, and black has the toastiest flavor and a crunchier texture. When quinoa first became popular outside of South America, there was concern about the environmental impact of quinoa production, but the consensus is that quinoa is sustainable and that any unfair labor practices involved in cultivating it are no worse than other crops—so like other purchases, try to support fair-trade producers.

Buckwheat is another pseudograin. Long popular in Asia and Eastern Europe, buckwheat groats (the edible seed part of the plant) are becoming more widely appreciated here, probably because buckwheat is gluten-free and certainly because of its robust, nutty flavor. Chia is another pseudocereal that I use more sparingly, such as sprinkled atop a spa salad for a dose of protein, minerals, and omega-3 fatty acids.

Other seeds featured atop the salads in this chapter (and other chapters too) are pumpkin, hemp, sunflower, sesame, and poppy—all crunchy, tasty, and nutritious additions.

quinoa, spring vegetables, arugula, kumquats, pistachios

6 SERVINGS / GF

I have pretty kumquat trees on my terrace. I'll pluck and pop one of the little orange citrus into my mouth whenever I walk by for a quick, puckering pick-me-up. Kumquats are a great addition to salad—the peel is sweet, and the pulp adds the perfect amount of tart. When I've eaten all the kumquats off my tree, I use tangerine sections, which are good in this salad too.

1½ cups water

½ teaspoon salt, plus more to taste

1 cup quinoa

4 ounces feta cheese, crumbled

¼ cup chopped fresh herbs, such as dill, mint, and/or cilantro

6 tablespoons extra-virgin olive oil

3 tablespoons fresh lemon juice

6 ounces sugar snap peas, trimmed

4 tablespoons Champagne vinegar or white wine vinegar

2 cups wild or baby arugula

2 carrots, very thinly sliced

1 fennel bulb, trimmed and very thinly sliced

12 kumquats, sliced, or 4 tangerines, peeled and separated into sections

2 watermelon radishes, peeled and very thinly sliced

½ cup shelled roasted pistachios

Bring the water and salt to a simmer in a heavy small saucepan over medium heat. Add the quinoa, cover, and simmer until the liquid has been absorbed and the quinoa is tender, about 20 minutes. Transfer the quinoa to a large bowl, fluff with a fork, and cool completely. Add the cheese, herbs, 2 tablespoons of the oil, and the lemon juice to the quinoa and stir to combine. Season with salt and pepper.

Meanwhile, cook the snap peas in a medium pot of rapidly boiling salted water until crisp-tender. Drain well. *(The quinoa and snap peas can be prepared up to 2 days ahead; cover and refrigerate separately.)*

Whisk together the remaining 4 tablespoons oil, the vinegar, and ¼ teaspoon salt to blend in a small bowl for the dressing. Mix the snap peas, arugula, carrots, fennel, kumquats, radishes, and pistachios into the quinoa mixture. Toss with the dressing and serve.

Tip: I use an inexpensive V-slicer to shave paper-thin slices of the fennel, carrot, and watermelon radish.

roasted spiced carrots, quinoa, chickpeas, green ribbons, turmeric vinaigrette

4 SERVINGS / GF

Roasting brings out the best in carrots—the flavor deepens, and the texture becomes tender with a pleasant, dare I say "meaty" bite. I could make an entire meal of just these roasted carrots, but adding turmeric-infused quinoa and chickpeas, ribbons of dark green kale, dried cherries, and a lemony vinaigrette really elevates this root. Look for tender, organic carrots (organic carrots tend to be sweeter) that are ½ to ¾ inch in diameter. If only larger carrots are available, cut them into ½-inch-thick strips. I like the salad with garlicky yogurt, but it's also excellent as is.

1½ cups water

2 teaspoons ground turmeric

½ teaspoon salt, plus more to taste

1 cup quinoa

1 (14- to 16-ounce) can chickpeas, rinsed and drained

6 tablespoons extra-virgin olive oil, plus more for brushing

1 shallot, finely chopped (about a scant ½ cup)

⅓ cup fresh lemon juice

2 garlic cloves, finely grated or crushed with a garlic press

Freshly ground black pepper

1 small bunch lacinato kale or mustard greens, center ribs removed, leaves cut into thin ribbons (about 3 cups lightly packed)

½ cup dried sour cherries, currants, or golden raisins

2 bunches thin carrots (about 1¼ pounds)

1 rounded teaspoon cumin seeds

1 rounded teaspoon fennel seeds

1 scant teaspoon red pepper flakes

2 cups baby arugula leaves

Aleppo pepper, for sprinkling

Garlicky Yogurt (page 215)

Roasted hulled sunflower seeds (optional)

Bring the water, 1 teaspoon of the turmeric, and the salt to a simmer in a heavy small saucepan over medium heat. Add the quinoa, cover, and simmer until the liquid has been absorbed and the quinoa is tender, about 20 minutes. Fluff the quinoa with a fork, mix in the chickpeas, and cool completely. *(The quinoa mixture can be prepared up to 3 days ahead; cover and refrigerate.)*

Preheat the oven to 425°F.

Whisk together 4 tablespoons of the oil with the shallot, lemon juice, garlic, and remaining 1 teaspoon turmeric in a small bowl for the dressing. Season generously with salt and black pepper.

recipe continues

In a large bowl, combine the kale with 1 tablespoon of the remaining oil and massage gently with your hands to tenderize the kale. Add the quinoa mixture and sour cherries to the kale and toss well.

Brush a heavy large sheet pan with oil. Toss the carrots with the remaining 1 tablespoon oil on the prepared sheet pan and spread out evenly. Sprinkle the carrots with the cumin seeds, fennel seeds, and red pepper flakes. Sprinkle lightly with salt. Roast the carrots until tender and browned on the edges, stirring and rotating the position in the oven once, about 18 minutes.

Meanwhile, whisk the dressing to blend, pour it over the quinoa mixture, then add the arugula and toss well. Transfer the salad to a platter. Top with the carrots, scraping any spices from the pan onto the salad. Sprinkle with Aleppo pepper. Serve with garlicky yogurt and a scattering of sunflower seeds, if desired.

QUINOA: TO RINSE OR NOT TO RINSE?

Living in a drought-stricken area, I've adapted my kitchen habits to be very water-wise. When I wash salad greens, I dump the water from my spinner onto my plants. Likewise, when I boil things like eggs or soak beans, that water also goes into the garden. Even though I know that my conservation efforts add up to a literal drop in the bucket, it makes me feel better. So, when a recipe or package says that quinoa should be rinsed "until the water runs clear," I wonder if I really need to. The answer depends on the brand. Quinoa seeds grow their own insect repellent, saponin, a naturally occurring coating that can impart the bitter flavor, hence the call to rinse. Some brands, including Bob's Red Mill, sell quinoa that has been "prewashed" to remove the saponin. Prewashed quinoa has in fact not been rinsed but has been slightly abraded to remove the thin bitter coating. If you don't want to rinse, look for the prewashed variety.

acorn squash, wilted red cabbage, apple, pumpkin seed dressing

3 TO 4 SERVINGS / GF, VEGAN OPTION

I have never been to Austria except in my imagination. In that idyll, a white-tablecloth restaurant with a glorious view and plenty of vegetarian menu options would serve this as their specialty. In keeping with the setting, accompany the salad with sourdough rye and chilled Grüner Veltliner. Because we're on holiday, why not finish with Linzer torte, Sachertorte, or strudel. Mâche is a tender baby lettuce often called lamb's lettuce. It's getting harder and harder to find, so watercress makes for a good green addition.

Dressing

½ cup raw cashew pieces

½ cup water

2 tablespoons pumpkin seed oil

1 tablespoon apple cider vinegar

1 small garlic clove, peeled

1 teaspoon honey or maple syrup

½ teaspoon salt , plus more for sprinkling

1 green onion, white and green parts kept separate, thinly sliced

Salad

1 acorn squash (about 1½ pounds), seeded and cut into 12 wedges

2 tablespoons extra-virgin olive oil

1 teaspoon paprika

2 teaspoons salt, plus more for roasting the squash

Honey or maple syrup (about 1 tablespoon), for drizzling

6 cups thinly sliced cored red cabbage (about ½ small head)

2 cups boiling water

1 tablespoon apple cider vinegar

1 tart green apple

2 cups mâche (lamb's lettuce or field lettuce) or watercress

Toasted pepitas (shelled pumpkin seeds), for sprinkling

For the dressing: Soak the cashews in the water in a small bowl for at least 2 hours or overnight. Transfer the cashews and water to a blender along with the oil, vinegar, garlic, honey, and salt. Add the green parts of the onion (reserve the white and pale green parts) and blend until very smooth. *(The dressing can be prepared up to 4 days ahead. Cover and refrigerate.)*

For the salad: Preheat the oven to 400°F.

Toss the squash with 1 tablespoon of the oil and the paprika on a heavy large sheet pan. Sprinkle with some salt and roast for 10 minutes. Turn the squash and roast until tender when pierced with a knife, about 10 minutes longer. Arrange the squash slices skin-side down and close together. Drizzle with honey. Return the squash to the oven and roast until glazed, about 3 minutes.

recipe continues

Meanwhile: Combine the cabbage and 2 teaspoons salt in a large bowl. Pour the boiling water over the cabbage and let stand for 30 minutes to 1 hour. Drain the cabbage, gently squeezing out any excess moisture. Transfer the cabbage to a bowl and toss with the remaining 1 tablespoon oil, the vinegar, and the white and light green parts of the green onion.

To serve: Divide the cabbage among plates. Using a V-slicer or mandoline, thinly slice the apple into rounds and scatter the rounds over the cabbage. Divide the squash among plates. Drizzle with dressing, sprinkle with the mâche and pepitas, and serve.

Note: Pumpkin seed oil is a dark green and very flavorful finishing oil. It's cold-pressed from Austrian Styrian pumpkin seeds. The oil is purported to have several benefits, including hair growth, breast firming, and prostate health, but I love it for its toasty rich flavor. La Tourangelle sells a very good one in specialty foods stores and online.

ROASTED SQUASH MIX AND MATCH

Slices or cubes of roasted squash are a colorful, seasonal way to bring flavor and nutrition to fall salads. The sweetness of the squash melds well with the gentle acid of vinaigrettes and dressings. If you garden or are blessed with the remnants of an autumn table cornucopia, you might find yourself with an abundance of, say, delicata, acorn, sweet dumpling, red kuri, butternut, or kabocha squash. Because there are so many orange-fleshed winter squash varieties to choose from, you can substitute one squash for another in the salads in this book. If you plan to swap out squash, simply check the weight measurement in the recipe and use that as your guide to end up with an appropriate amount of squash for the salad.

grilled sweet potatoes, kale, garlicky yogurt, puffed buckwheat

4 SERVINGS / GF

Buckwheat groats can be "popped," transforming them into a crunchy and nutritious addition to salads. This recipe has a few convenient do-aheads, making it great for weeknight menu planning. Russian kale is excellent for grilling, as the leaves are flat and the edges don't curl from the grill to the fire, but as it's less common, any kale will do—just take extra care to avoid charcoal edges.

2 pounds dark-fleshed sweet potatoes (about 4 thin)	2 pounds kale, preferably Russian kale (about 2 bunches)	Garlicky Yogurt (page 215)
Salt	Extra-virgin olive oil	Aleppo pepper
6 tablespoons roasted buckwheat groats (kasha)	Freshly ground black pepper	

Cook the sweet potatoes in a large pot of rapidly boiling salted water until almost tender when pierced with a thin, sharp knife, about 15 minutes. Drain and cool completely.

Set a large bowl next to the stove. Heat a heavy large skillet over high heat. Pour about 2 tablespoons of the groats into the skillet and stir continuously until the groats puff or pop, 30 seconds to 1 minute. Immediately transfer the puffed groats to the bowl. Repeat the process two more times until all the groats are puffed. *(The sweet potatoes and buckwheat can be prepared up to 2 days ahead. Refrigerate the sweet potatoes; cover and seal the buckwheat in an airtight container and store at room temperature.)*

Heat a grill to medium. Working in batches, arrange the kale leaves in a single layer on the grill and cook until just wilted, 30 seconds to 1 minute. Turn the kale and cook until the leaves are tender and very lightly charred at the edges, 30 seconds to 1 minute longer. (Some of the leaves may not need turning, depending on the heat of the grill.) Transfer the kale to a large platter. Maintain the grill temperature.

Using a sharp knife, cut the sweet potatoes lengthwise into quarters. Brush the sweet potatoes with oil and season with salt and pepper. Grill the sweet potatoes until browned on all sides, turning occasionally, about 10 minutes.

Arrange the kale and the sweet potatoes on a platter or serving plates and top with a generous drizzling of garlicky yogurt. Sprinkle with the puffed buckwheat and Aleppo pepper and serve.

red quinoa and red kidney bean masala

4 TO 6 SERVINGS / GF, VEGAN

Rajma is a casual bean curry that's popular throughout India. Inspired by that dish, I combined red kidney beans and red quinoa with Indian flavors including tamarind, ginger, mint, and cilantro to make this delightfully interpretive masala, or spicy mix. I added roasted peanuts and chickpea snacks for fun crunch. You can serve the salad with warm naan and yogurt for a big dinner.

Quinoa

1 cup red or tricolor quinoa

2 cups water

½ teaspoon salt

Dressing

¼ cup peanut oil, untoasted (light) sesame oil, or other neutral oil

¼ cup fresh lime or lemon juice

2 teaspoons finely grated fresh ginger (about a 1-inch piece)

2 garlic cloves, finely grated or crushed with a garlic press

½ teaspoon salt

Salad

2 (14- to 16-ounce) cans red kidney beans, rinsed and drained

1 hothouse cucumber, quartered and sliced

2 cups cherry tomatoes, cut in half

½ red onion, diced

¼ cup minced fresh cilantro leaves, plus whole leaves (optional) for garnish

¼ cup minced fresh mint leaves, plus whole leaves (optional) for garnish

1 serrano chile, stemmed, seeded, and minced

1 (6-ounce) package Bombay Spice or other crunchy, spicy, Indian-style snack mix (about 2 cups)

¾ cup (or more) lightly salted roasted peanuts

Tamarind Chutney Sauce (page 215)

Bring the water, quinoa, and salt to a boil in a heavy medium saucepan over medium-high heat. Reduce the heat to medium and simmer until the quinoa is tender and the water is absorbed, about 15 minutes. Remove from the heat, cover, and let stand until cool. Transfer the quinoa to a large bowl.

For the dressing: Whisk together the oil, lime juice, ginger, garlic, and salt to blend in a small bowl.

For the salad: Stir the beans, cucumber, tomatoes, red onion, cilantro, mint, and chile into the quinoa along with the dressing.

To serve: Spoon the salad onto plates and sprinkle generously with crunchy chickpeas and peanuts. Drizzle with tamarind chutney sauce, garnish with mint and cilantro leaves, if desired, and serve.

coconut quinoa, black beans, avocado, mango, collards, plantain, cashews

4 SERVINGS / GF, VEGAN

Simmering quinoa in coconut milk makes it rich and slightly sweet. Cooled, I combine it with Brazilian favorites including black beans, collard greens, mango, avocado, and cashews for a beachy meal. Raw collard greens, just like raw kale, are tasty in salads, and unlike kale, thin ribbons of collards don't require a tenderizing massage.

Coconut Quinoa

1 (13- to 14-ounce) can unsweetened coconut milk

¾ cup quinoa

¼ teaspoon salt

Dressing

⅓ cup fresh lime juice

2 tablespoons peanut or other neutral oil

¼ teaspoon ground allspice

¼ teaspoon salt

Salad

1 (14- to 16-ounce) can black beans, rinsed and drained

1 to 1½ cups diced mango (about 1 mango)

1 yellow or orange bell pepper, diced, or 4 mini bell peppers, sliced

½ small red onion, halved and sliced

1 large jalapeño chile, stemmed, seeded, and diced

4 cups thinly sliced stemmed collard greens (about 1 bunch) or baby spinach leaves

2 avocados, sliced

¾ cup roasted and salted cashew pieces

Plantain chips, for garnish (optional)

Unsweetened coconut flakes, for garnish (optional)

Lime wedges

For the coconut quinoa: Whisk the coconut milk, quinoa, and salt together in a heavy small saucepan. Bring to a simmer over medium-high heat. Reduce the heat to medium-low and simmer until the quinoa resembles pudding, about 20 minutes. Cover, turn off the heat, and let stand until cool.

For the dressing: Whisk together the lime juice, oil, allspice, and salt in a small bowl.

For the salad: Transfer the quinoa to a large bowl and fluff with a fork. Add the black beans, mango, bell pepper, onion, and jalapeño to the quinoa. Pour over half the dressing and toss to combine. *(The salad can be made up to this point up to 6 hours ahead; cover and refrigerate.)*

Carefully mix in the collard greens. Spoon the salad onto plates and top with the avocado. Drizzle with the remaining dressing. Sprinkle with the cashews and, if desired, plantain chips and coconut flakes. Serve with lime wedges.

Tip: If good mangoes are hard to find where you live, the solution can be found in the freezer in the form of packaged frozen organic mango pieces. Simply thaw the amount you want and the fruit is always perfectly sweet, smooth and not stringy. If you can get your hands on good-quality fresh mangoes, use those.

black quinoa, black lentils, pomegranate, orange, honey-baked feta

6 SERVINGS / GF

Here is my interpretation of a memorable citrus-adorned salad I enjoyed on the island of Hydra in Greece. The hearty seed-and-pulse salad features baked feta, but if time is short, it's good with crumbled feta too. Pour a chilled assyrtiko to enjoy with the meal. Any leftovers can be refreshed with a squeeze of orange or tangerine juice.

Quinoa and Lentils

8 cups water

1 scant teaspoon salt

1 bay leaf

1½ cups black or tricolor quinoa, rinsed and drained

¾ cup dried French or black lentils

Salad

1½ teaspoons cumin seeds

½ cup extra-virgin olive oil, plus more for drizzling

¼ cup plus 2 tablespoons fresh lemon juice

⅓ cup finely chopped shallot

1 tablespoon honey, plus more for drizzling

1 large garlic clove, finely grated or crushed with a garlic press

1 generous teaspoon ground cinnamon

1 teaspoon ground turmeric

½ teaspoon salt

1 cup pomegranate seeds

⅓ cup chopped fresh Italian parsley

1 pound feta cheese, cut into ¾-inch-thick slices

1 small head lettuce, torn into 3- to 4-inch pieces, rinsed, and gently spun dry

6 small oranges or tangerines, peeled and sliced

For the quinoa and lentils: Bring the water, salt, and bay leaf to a boil in a heavy large saucepan over medium-high heat. Add the quinoa and lentils, return to a boil, and cook until tender, about 20 minutes. Drain the quinoa mixture well.

For the salad: Stir the cumin seeds in a heavy small dry skillet over medium-high heat until fragrant and lightly toasted, about 1 minute. Remove from the heat.

Whisk together ½ cup of the oil, the lemon juice, shallot, honey, garlic, cinnamon, turmeric, and salt in a large bowl until blended. Stir in the cumin seeds. Add the quinoa mixture, pomegranate seeds, and parsley and stir gently to combine. (*The salad can be prepared up to this point up to 3 days ahead; cover and refrigerate.*)

Preheat the oven or a toaster oven to 400°F.

Brush a shallow baking dish with olive oil. Arrange the cheese in the prepared dish. Brush the cheese with oil. Bake until the cheese is just browned at the edges, about 10 minutes. Drizzle the cheese with honey.

Gently massage the lettuce with just enough oil and salt to barely coat in another large bowl. Add the lentil mixture and oranges and toss gently just to combine. Serve the salad topped with the baked honey cheese.

beet, buckwheat, walnuts, greens, goat gouda

4 SERVINGS / GF

Most people know buckwheat as flour, sifted into blueberry pancakes, but pre-ground groats are worth knowing. Buckwheat is a pseudocereal—a seed that is playing the part of a grain. The "groat" is the hulled seed of the plant. Protein- and iron-rich groats are a staple in Eastern Europe, commonly served boiled into a porridge. Here earthy buckwheat is highlighted by sweet beets, robust walnuts, and nutty goat Gouda, and it's gluten-free. Be sure to purchase a roasted or toasted groat, such as Biorina.

Beets

1 pound beets (about 6 small to medium), a few leafy greens reserved if possible

Extra virgin olive or vegetable oil, for drizzling

Buckwheat

1¾ cups water

1 cup roasted buckwheat groats (kasha)

¼ teaspoon salt

Dressing

⅓ cup walnut or extra-virgin olive oil

¼ cup apple cider vinegar

2 tablespoons honey

¼ cup finely chopped shallot

1 garlic clove, finely grated or crushed with a garlic press

½ teaspoon salt

Salad

1 large green apple, thinly sliced

1 cup coarsely grated goat's-milk Gouda cheese

½ cup thin slices tender beet greens or Swiss chard leaves

½ cup walnut pieces, toasted

Lettuce leaves, for serving (optional)

For the beets: Preheat the oven to 375°F.

Arrange the beets in a small baking dish, drizzle with a little oil, and turn the beets to coat them with oil. Cover the baking dish with foil. Bake until the beets are tender when pierced with a thin knife, about 45 minutes. Set aside to cool completely. *(The beets can be prepared up to 1 week ahead. Cover the baking dish with plastic wrap and refrigerate.)*

For the buckwheat: Bring the water, buckwheat, and salt to a boil in a heavy small saucepan over high heat. Reduce the heat to medium, cover, and simmer until the liquid has been absorbed and the buckwheat is tender, about 12 minutes. Transfer the buckwheat to a large bowl and cool.

For the dressing: Whisk together all the ingredients to blend in a small bowl.

For the salad: Peel, trim, and slice the beets. Add the beets to the buckwheat along with the apple, cheese, beet greens, and walnuts. Pour the dressing over the salad and toss gently. Season with additional salt, if necessary, and black pepper. Serve as is or on lettuce-lined plates, if desired.

kohlrabi, avocado, egg, radicchio, watercress, mustard-poppy vinaigrette

2 SERVINGS / GF

Kohrabi, a member of the cabbage family, can be cooked or eaten raw in salads or slaws. The flavor is like broccoli stem but milder and sweeter—it's great with the slightly bitter radicchio, creamy avocado, and rich eggs.

2 eggs

3 tablespoons extra-virgin olive oil

2 tablespoons white wine vinegar

1 tablespoon Dijon mustard

1 tablespoon poppy seeds

¼ teaspoon salt

8 radicchio or Treviso leaves

1 bunch watercress, trimmed (about 2 cups)

8 ounces kohlrabi, trimmed, peeled, and cut into matchstick-sized pieces

1 large avocado, sliced

Freshly ground black pepper

Cover the eggs with water in a medium saucepan and bring to a gentle simmer. Simmer the eggs for 5 minutes. Remove from the heat; cover and let stand for 5 minutes. Remove the eggs from the water and rinse with cold water to cool. Refrigerate until well chilled. *(The eggs can be cooked up to 1 week ahead and refrigerated.)*

Whisk together the oil, vinegar, mustard, poppy seeds, and salt to blend in a small bowl for the dressing. Layer the radicchio, watercress, kohlrabi, and avocado in a large shallow bowl or on a platter. Peel and chop the eggs and add them to the salad. Drizzle the dressing over the salad, top with black pepper, and serve.

POPPY SEEDS

It's hard to imagine how the ancient Egyptians first discovered the culinary application of the poppy seed. The same seed that comes from opium poppy pods has a delicate, sweet, and nutty flavor and a pleasant "popping" bite. Poppy seeds speckle cakes and pastries, breads, buns, and egg noodles in Eastern European and Middle Eastern cooking, and in Indian cuisine they can be used as a way to thicken sauces. Most recipes use the seeds modestly, but hamantaschen, the tricornered pastries that are part of the Jewish holiday Purim, are filled with a thick, sweet paste made from loads of poppy seeds and sugar. There's a Turkish cake that calls for so many poppy seeds in the batter that the resulting crumb is bluish purple. In the U.S., cooks began to add poppy seeds to salad dressing in the '50s to add tiny crunch and as a gentle emulsifier. Note of caution: Eating poppy seeds less than 48 hours before a drug test can lead to a positive result.

heirloom salad, creamy sesame-miso tofu

4 SERVINGS / GF OPTION, VEGAN

The tart, lightly dressed greens meld well with the creamy bed of miso and sesame-flavored tofu. When tomatoes are in season, they make a lovely addition to the mix. You can serve the salad with Japanese crackers for a fun bit of crunch.

Sesame-Miso Tofu

1 (14-ounce) package firm tofu

⅓ cup white miso paste

3 tablespoons rice vinegar

3 tablespoons toasted sesame seeds

Dressing

3 tablespoons untoasted (light) sesame oil or other neutral oil

3 tablespoons rice vinegar

1 tablespoon soy sauce or tamari

1 teaspoon toasted sesame oil

¾ teaspoon sugar

Salad

4 cups heirloom green mix, preferably mizuna, tatsoi, and oakleaf

1 Japanese, hothouse, or Persian cucumber, very thinly sliced

1 medium watermelon radish, very thinly sliced

2 medium heirloom tomatoes, cut into wedges (optional)

Toasted sesame seeds, for garnish

For the tofu: Place the tofu in a colander and set over the sink or a bowl. Place a clean cereal bowl on top of the tofu as a weight and let drain for 1 hour.

Using a handheld or conventional blender, blend the tofu, miso, vinegar, and sesame seeds until smooth. Transfer the mixture to a bowl and chill. *(The tofu can be prepared up to 4 days ahead; cover and refrigerate.)*

For the dressing: Whisk together the ingredients to blend in a small bowl. *(The tofu and dressing can be prepared up to 4 days ahead; cover and keep refrigerated.)*

To serve the salad: Combine the greens with the cucumber, radish, and tomatoes, if using, in a large bowl. Spoon and spread the miso-tofu mixture onto plates. Whisk the dressing to blend; add enough dressing to coat the salad lightly. Top the miso tofu with the salad. Sprinkle with sesame seeds and serve.

spa salad with seeds, free-free dressing

2 TO 4 SERVINGS / GF, VEGAN

Hemp and chia seeds are high in omega fatty acids and protein and are quite tasty in this mix of cruciferous vegetables, cleansing apples and carrots, and more nutrient-rich seeds and almonds tossed in a sweetly satisfying dressing. I call the dressing "free-free" because it's fat-free and sugar-free. This salad is great freshly tossed, but overnight it takes on new qualities—the vegetables and fruit soften slightly, and the seeds moisten and plump with the dressing and coat every bite, making it a great option for a meal on the go. Make it when you feel you need a dietary reset.

1 large stalk broccoli (about ½ bunch)

1 bunch lacinato kale, center rib removed, leaves thinly sliced (about 4 cups)

1 tart green apple, cored and cut into matchstick-sized pieces

1 carrot, grated

⅓ cup roasted and salted sunflower seeds

¼ cup raw or toasted almonds, finely chopped

¼ cup dried cranberries, preferably unsweetened, chopped

¼ cup hulled hemp seeds (optional)

2 tablespoons chia seeds

2 tablespoons toasted sesame seeds

Free-Free Dressing (recipe follows)

Trim and peel the stem of the broccoli. Cut the stem and florets into ½-inch pieces. (You should have about 2 cups.) Combine the broccoli, kale, apple, carrot, sunflower seeds, almonds, cranberries, hemp seeds, chia seeds, and sesame seeds to blend in a large bowl. Add the dressing and toss well. *(The salad can be prepared up to 2 days ahead. Cover and refrigerate.)*

free-free dressing

MAKES ABOUT 1½ CUPS

The dressing gets its sweetness from pineapple. I use frozen pineapple for convenience's sake, but fresh works too. I store ginger in my freezer, a trick I learned from my sister. To use, simply grate the frozen root with a fine Microplane-style grater and return the unused portion to the freezer.

10 ounces frozen pineapple chunks (about 1¼ cups), thawed

⅓ cup rice vinegar

¼ cup mellow white miso paste

1 (1¼-inch-thick) slice fresh ginger, or 1 generous teaspoon grated fresh ginger

Blend the ingredients in a blender until smooth. Transfer to a jar and keep refrigerated for up to 1 week.

pasta salads

Pasta encompasses not only the classic Italian staple, but noodles and pastas from Asia—soba, somen, and rice noodles, as well as semolina couscous ranging from the fine North African style to the larger Israeli couscous and Sardinian fregola. The salads in this section tend toward the Mediterranean and Asian styles made with durum wheat and buckwheat. Salads with rice noodles are featured elsewhere in this book.

Pasta salads became all the rage in the 1980s and '90s. The ease of serving a room-temperature or cold pasta dish is indisputable. Noodles adapt easily to whatever goodies one might have, and are relatively inexpensive and readily available at the local supermarket, so it's easy to understand the popularity. Unfortunately, bottled "Italian" dressing, overcooked fusilli, and soggy additions became the norm, and pasta salad fell out of favor. I'd like to think the recipes in this chapter will redeem the pasta salad and return it to good graces in your home.

pesto zoodles and noodles

SERVES 4 TO 6

I must admit, when I first heard about the produce-spiral-cutting gadget, I thought it was a silly gimmick. But when I had to buy a spiralizer for an assignment, my kitchen counter and garden just happened to be covered with zucchini, and I became an instant "zoodle" (zucchini noodle) convert. I like to combine zoodles with whole wheat spaghetti for structure and substance, but you can replace the spaghetti with more zoodles for a grain-free dish or use another type of semolina pasta.

8 ounces whole wheat spaghetti

Salt

8 tablespoons extra-virgin olive oil

3 garlic cloves, finely grated or crushed with a garlic press

2½ pounds zucchini (about 2 medium)

¼ cup white wine vinegar

1 cup coarsely grated Parmesan cheese

½ cup packed fresh basil leaves, thinly sliced

½ cup pine nuts, toasted

Freshly ground black pepper

Cook the spaghetti in a medium pot of rapidly boiling salted water until al dente. Drain the spaghetti and transfer it to a large bowl. Immediately toss with 1 tablespoon of the oil and one-third of the garlic.

Meanwhile, cut the zucchini into spaghetti-sized zoodles with a spiralizer. Add the zoodles to the spaghetti along with the remaining oil and garlic.

When ready to serve, pour over the vinegar, add the cheese, basil, and pine nuts, and toss to combine. Season the salad with salt and pepper and serve.

Tip: If you don't want to acquire another kitchen tool, you can cut the zucchini into thin noodle-shaped pieces instead. Trim the zucchini. Hold the zucchini on the cutting board with the stem side toward you. Using a large sharp knife, cut a thin slice off the long edge of the zucchini. Turn the zucchini so that the cut side rests on the cutting board and the stem end still faces you. Slice the zucchini into ⅛- to ¼-inch-thick slices. Stack the slices and cut into ⅛- to ¼-inch-wide strips.

buckwheat soba, kabocha squash, walnuts, persimmon, greens

2 SERVINGS / GF OPTION, VEGAN

Buckwheat soba means "buckwheat buckwheat," as *soba* is Japanese for "buckwheat."

The earthy flavor of the soba pairs well with walnuts. This noodle salad features sherry-simmered kabocha squash, but it's great with any kind of cooked winter squash, be it roasted butternut, acorn, or delicata.

3 tablespoons sherry

1 tablespoon sugar

3 tablespoons rice vinegar

1½ tablespoons soy sauce or tamari

1 (3.5-ounce) bundle soba (Japanese buckwheat noodles)

1½ tablespoons toasted sesame oil

1½ cups cubed cooked kabocha or other winter squash (recipe follows)

1 cup thinly sliced lacinato kale leaves

1 cup mixed Japanese salad greens, such as mizuna and tatsoi

1 Fuyu persimmon or Asian apple pear, diced

⅓ cup walnuts, coarsely ground or very finely chopped

2 tablespoons toasted black sesame seeds

Combine the sherry and sugar in a small saucepan and stir over medium-low heat just until the sugar dissolves and the alcohol dissipates. Remove from the heat, cool slightly, and stir in the vinegar and soy sauce or tamari.

Bring a large saucepan of water to a boil. Add the noodles and stir briefly to prevent clumping. Boil until just tender, about 5 minutes. Meanwhile, fill a large bowl with cold water. Drain the noodles and add to the cold water. Gently swish the noodles in the water to rinse and cool. Drain the noodles well and transfer to another large bowl; gently stir in the sesame oil.

Add the squash, kale, greens, persimmon, walnuts, and sesame seeds and toss gently. Divide the salad between two plates and serve with the dressing.

Tip: Want extra protein? Consider adding a Soy Egg (page 30) or a slice of soft tofu.

recipe continues

sherry-simmered kabocha squash

Kabocha is a deep orange, dense, and sweet winter squash that is very popular in Japan. With edible skin, it's vitamin- and fiber-rich and very filling. Mirin, a sweet, rice-based cooking wine, flavors the braising liquid in Japanese recipes, but I use sherry. You can use either. Enjoy the cold squash as is with a sprinkle of sesame seeds or add it to salads or soups.

1 small kabocha squash (about 2 pounds)

2 cups water

1 tablespoon sherry

1 tablespoon honey or agave nectar

1 tablespoon soy sauce or tamari

Cut the squash into quarters from stem to tail end. Remove the seeds. Cut the squash quarters in half crosswise, then cut each piece in half, forming two wedges. Arrange the squash pieces, skin-side down, in a heavy pot that is just large enough to fit them in one layer. Pour in the water, sherry, honey, and soy sauce or tamari and swirl gently to combine. Bring the squash mixture to a simmer over medium-low heat. Cover and simmer until the squash is just tender when pierced with a thin, sharp knife, about 12 minutes. Remove from the heat. Carefully transfer the squash to a bowl. Reserve the cooking liquid and cool completely. Pour the cooking liquid over the squash and chill. *(The squash can be prepared up to 5 days ahead. Cover and keep refrigerated.)*

saffron gem couscous, smashed cucumbers with mint, greens, pomegranate vinaigrette

4 TO 6 SERVINGS

Barberries resemble small red raisins and are quite sour. In Persian, they are called *zereshk*. Look for them at Middle Eastern or Persian markets or simply use chopped dried sour cherries in their place. The components of this salad can be prepared ahead, making it ideal for picnics or entertaining.

Couscous

2½ cups water

3 tablespoons extra-virgin olive oil

2 garlic cloves, finely grated or crushed with a garlic press

1 teaspoon salt, plus more to taste

¼ teaspoon saffron threads

2 cups couscous (about 10 ounces)

½ cup barberries or chopped pitted dried sour cherries

⅓ cup golden raisins

¼ cup chopped dried apricots

3 green onions, thinly sliced

½ cup mixed chopped fresh herbs, such as dill, cilantro, and Italian parsley

Freshly ground black pepper

Vinaigrette

2 tablespoons apple cider vinegar

2 tablespoons pomegranate concentrate or pomegranate molasses

2 tablespoons extra-virgin olive oil

¼ teaspoon salt

1 to 2 teaspoons honey

Salad

4 to 6 cups mixed greens, such as baby spinach, arugula, and oakleaf lettuce

Smashed Cucumbers with Mint (recipe follows)

¾ cup sliced almonds, toasted

For the couscous: Bring the water, oil, garlic, salt, and saffron to a boil in a heavy medium saucepan. Remove the pan from the heat; stir in the couscous. Cover and let stand for 5 minutes. Fluff with a fork, then transfer to a large bowl. Immediately add the barberries, raisins, and apricots. Cool slightly. Stir in the green onions and herbs and season with salt and pepper. *(The couscous can be prepared up to 1 day ahead; cover and refrigerate. Let come to room temperature before serving.)*

For the vinaigrette: Whisk together the vinegar, pomegranate concentrate or molasses, oil, and salt to blend in a small bowl. Add honey to sweeten to taste. *(The vinaigrette can be prepared up to 1 day ahead. Cover and refrigerate.)*

Line a platter or plates with greens and top with the couscous. Follow with the smashed cucumbers and drizzle with the vinaigrette. Sprinkle with the almonds and serve.

recipe continues

smashed cucumbers with mint

Bruising and breaking up cucumbers with a blunt instrument might seem like a peculiar cooking technique, but "smashing" cucumbers tenderizes and sweetens the cukes by releasing seeds and breaking the skin. The resulting randomly sized chunks, once salted, drained, and chilled, are refreshingly pleasant to eat. We can thank the Chinese for the original veggie smashing, but the technique has been adopted worldwide. You can wrap your cucumbers in plastic wrap before whacking them to prevent errant bits and drips from flying about the kitchen.

6 Persian cucumbers

1 scant teaspoon salt

¾ cup plain Greek yogurt
or labneh

½ cup fresh mint leaves

Place the cucumbers on a cutting board and smack firmly yet gently with the side of a chef's knife, slightly crushing and breaking them into large chunks. Thickly slice any large pieces of cucumber and transfer to a colander. Sprinkle with the salt, toss well, and set over a bowl to drain, about 20 minutes. Stir in the yogurt and mint. *(The cucumbers can be prepared up to 1 day ahead. Cover and refrigerate.)*

POMEGRANATE MOLASSES AND POMEGRANATE CONCENTRATE

Pomegranate molasses and pomegranate concentrate are bottled syrups from the Middle East. The former is used mostly in savory foods while the latter is more suited for use in sweets and as a beverage syrup (think natural grenadine). Pomegranate molasses is easier to find, but both make great additions to your salad pantry.

Pomegranate molasses is a dark brown, astringent syrup with a distinctive tart and tannic taste. Whole fruit, not just the plump, juicy seeds, are used in the reduction, along with added sugar and citric acid. The sweetness among brands varies, so taste and correct the seasoning with a little honey or agave syrup.

Pomegranate concentrate is simply reduced pomegranate juice. Some brands add berry skins to the mix to enhance the color. The hue is a pretty, deep magenta and the flavor is pure pomegranate. You can make your own by simmering 100% pomegranate juice until it is reduced to a syrup. If you don't care for the mouth-puckering punch of pomegranate molasses, use the concentrate instead.

fregola, fennel, olive, pecorino, orange, arugula

6 TO 8 SERVINGS

This salad is an ode to two Italian islands—Sardinia, from which hails fregola, a toasted semolina pasta, and Sicily, where fennel, orange, and olive salads are ubiquitous. This isn't an authentic dish—it's like a musical mash-up, recognizable yet new and very fun. Look for fregola at Italian markets or substitute giant toasted couscous.

Dressing

⅔ cup extra-virgin olive oil

2 teaspoons grated orange zest

½ cup fresh orange juice

⅓ cup fresh lemon juice

⅔ cup white wine vinegar

Salad

16 to 17.6 ounces fregola (according to package size)

Salt

Extra-virgin olive oil

2 medium fennel bulbs, trimmed and chopped (about 2½ cups)

¾ cup chopped pitted green olives, such as Cerignola or Castelvetrano (about 18)

¾ cup chopped red onion

4 cups wild or small arugula leaves

1¼ cups coarsely grated pecorino cheese

16 oil-cured black olives, pitted

¾ cup chopped roasted or toasted almonds

¼ cup chopped fennel fronds

4 oranges, peeled and sliced

For the dressing: Whisk together the ingredients to blend in a small bowl. *(The dressing can be prepared ahead. Cover and keep at cool room temperature for up to 4 hours or refrigerate overnight.)*

For the salad: Cook the fregola in rapidly boiling generously salted water until al dente. Drain well, but don't rinse. Transfer the fregola to a large bowl and toss gently with 1 tablespoon of the oil. Cool to room temperature. Stir in the fennel, green olives, and red onion. Pour half the dressing over the fregola and stir to combine. *(The fregola salad can be prepared ahead. Cover and keep at cool room temperature for up to 4 hours or refrigerate overnight.)*

Toss the arugula leaves in a large shallow bowl with enough of the remaining dressing to coat. Mix the cheese into the fregola and spoon the fregola atop the arugula in the bowl. Scatter the black olives, almonds, and fennel fronds over the fregola. Surround the arugula with the orange slices and serve with the remaining dressing.

artichoke with sambuca, pasta, ricotta salata

4 SERVINGS

A dear friend serves grilled baby artichokes doused with sambuca, an anise-flavored liqueur from Italy, at her parties. This salad is based on her signature dish and mixes lightly charred artichokes with the unexpected hint of licorice and freshly cooked pasta. For ease, frozen artichoke hearts can't be beat, but during spring, when tender baby artichokes are plentiful, this is a perfect way to enjoy them. Ricotta salata, available at some supermarkets, Italian delis, and cheese shops, is a firm, salty ricotta. It's milder and drier than feta and sweeter and moister than Parmesan, but either cheese can be substituted if you can't find ricotta salata.

¼ cup fresh lemon juice, plus 2 tablespoons if using fresh artichokes

2 pounds baby artichokes, or 2 (12-ounce) bags frozen artichoke hearts, thawed

⅓ cup plus 3 tablespoons extra-virgin olive oil

Salt

¼ cup Romana Sambuca or other anise-flavored liqueur (such as Pernod)

1 pound gemelli or other small pasta

2 garlic cloves, finely grated or crushed with a garlic press

½ cup fresh Italian parsley leaves

2 teaspoons lemon zest

4 ounces ricotta salata, grated (about ¾ cup)

Freshly ground black pepper

If using fresh artichokes, fill a bowl with cold water and add 2 tablespoons of the lemon juice. Peel back the outer leaves of each artichoke until the exposed leaves are tender and pale green. Trim off the tips and stems and cut the artichokes in half. Place the artichokes in the lemon water. (The artichokes can be prepared several hours ahead. To prevent oxidation, keep them in the lemon water until you're ready to continue.)

Preheat the oven to 450°F.

Drain the artichokes and pat dry. Toss with 2 tablespoons of the oil on a heavy sheet pan. Sprinkle the artichokes lightly with salt and roast until golden brown and tender when pierced with a knife, stirring once or twice, about 5 minutes for frozen or 15 minutes for fresh. Remove the artichokes from the oven; stir to turn and drizzle with the sambuca. Roast until well browned, about 5 minutes longer. Remove from the oven and cool.

Meanwhile, cook the pasta in a large pot of rapidly boiling heavily salted water until al dente. Drain well; do not rinse. Transfer the pasta to a large bowl; add 1 tablespoon of the oil and the garlic to the pasta and toss well. Cool to room temperature. Add the artichokes and parsley.

Whisk together the lemon zest, remaining ¼ cup lemon juice, and a very generous pinch of salt in a small bowl. Gradually whisk in the remaining ⅓ cup oil. Add the dressing and ricotta to the salad and toss to combine. Season with pepper and serve.

fava beans, asparagus, toasted couscous, spring herbs, preserved lemon, labneh

4 SERVINGS

We plant fava beans in our Southern California garden in late fall, and come spring, the plants start giving. This generous plant grows into tall stalks shaded with delicate, nutty-tasting leaves that make an excellent addition to the salad mix, and its pretty white butterfly flowers develop into pods that are entirely edible when pinkie-sized. Once matured, the large pods shuck to yield sweet, creamy-textured beans. The plant also sheds important nutrients into the soil. To truly enjoy eating fava beans, they should be double peeled, with the outer pod shucked and the inner shell removed by blanching. It's not difficult to double peel the beans, just time-consuming. The results are worth it, especially when mixed with crunchy raw asparagus and slightly chewy couscous. Toasted couscous is also sold as pearl or Israeli couscous.

2 pounds fava beans, shucked

Salt

2 tablespoons plus 2 teaspoons extra-virgin olive oil, plus more for drizzling

½ cup toasted (Israeli) couscous

2 cups water

1 bunch very thin asparagus (about 14 ounces), well-trimmed

2 tablespoons fresh lemon juice

3 tablespoons chopped Preserved Lemon (page 218)

1 to 1½ cups labneh

Aleppo pepper

¾ cup loosely packed mixed fresh herb leaves, such as dill, Italian parsley, and cilantro

Bring a large saucepan of salted water to a rapid boil. Add the fava beans and boil for 3 minutes. Drain and cool. Carefully peel away the thin white husks on the beans. *(You should have about 2 cups double-shelled fava beans.)*

Heat 2 teaspoons of the oil in a heavy medium saucepan over high heat. Add the couscous and stir until golden brown, about 2 minutes. Add the water and bring to a boil. Reduce the heat to medium and simmer until tender, about 10 minutes. Drain well, transfer to a medium bowl, and cool completely.

Using a sharp knife, cut the asparagus on a diagonal into ¼- to ½-inch-thick slices, leaving the tips intact. Stir the asparagus, fava beans, the remaining 2 tablespoons oil, the lemon juice, and 1 tablespoon of the preserved lemon into the couscous. *(This can be prepared up to 1 day ahead. Cover and refrigerate.)*

Spoon the labneh onto plates or bowls and surround with the couscous mixture. Sprinkle the labneh with the remaining 2 tablespoons preserved lemon and some Aleppo pepper. Drizzle the salads with oil, scatter the herbs over, and serve.

orecchiette, tomato-herb salsa cruda

4 SERVINGS

Salsa cruda, or raw sauce, showcases summer produce at its peak. I make this simple salad with tomatoes and herbs from the garden or farmers' market. The "little ear"–shaped noodles cup the goodies neatly. Be sure to use best-quality pasta and extra-virgin olive oil when preparing this dish.

1 pound mixed cherry or heirloom tomatoes, halved or chopped (about 3 cups)

¾ cup finely chopped mixed fresh herbs, such as basil, oregano, mint, Italian parsley, and chives

⅓ cup extra-virgin olive oil

2 tablespoons white wine vinegar

2 garlic cloves, finely grated or crushed with a garlic press

¼ teaspoon salt, plus more for cooking the pasta

Pinch of red pepper flakes

8 ounces orecchiette (ear-shaped pasta)

¾ cup coarsely grated Parmesan or Asiago cheese

Freshly ground black pepper

2 cups wild or baby arugula (optional)

Combine the tomatoes, herbs, oil, vinegar, garlic, salt, and red pepper flakes in a large bowl. *(This can be prepared ahead. Cover and let stand at cool room temperature for up to 6 hours.)*

Cook the pasta in a large pot of boiling salted water until it is tender but still firm to the bite, stirring occasionally. Drain. Add the pasta and cheese to the tomato mixture and season with pepper. Serve the salad warm or at room temperature, with a scattering of arugula, if desired.

Tip: I never rinse pasta even when making a salad. Noodles develop a starchy coating while boiling and this coating is what adheres sauces and flavors to the noodle. For my pasta salads I either mix the freshly cooked pasta directly into the sauce, or I toss it in olive oil and garlic right after draining to add flavor and keep the pasta from clumping.

OPPOSITE PAGE, CLOCKWISE FROM TOP: Loaded Orzo (page 159), Roasted Broccoli, Preserved Lemon, Calabrian Chile, Whole Wheat Pasta (page 158), and Orecchiette, Tomato-Herb Salsa Cruda (above)

roasted broccoli, preserved lemon, calabrian chile, whole wheat pasta

4 TO 6 SERVINGS / VEGAN / PHOTOGRAPH ON PAGE 157

Roasted cauliflower gets all the glory, but roasted broccoli deserves attention too. Savory and concentrated, tender with browned crunchy bits, salty with a little funky sweetness—it hits all the right notes. I combine roasted broccoli with other salty-tangy all-stars: preserved lemon and spicy fermented Calabrian chiles. As written, this salad is dairy-free, but it's also tasty with the addition of 6 ounces of crumbled feta cheese. If making the salad with feta, reduce the preserved lemon to 1 tablespoon, or replace with 1 teaspoon grated lemon zest. Whole wheat pasta is an acquired taste that works with this recipe. If you prefer another pasta, use it.

2 to 2½ pounds broccoli (about 2 bunches)

6 tablespoons extra-virgin olive oil, plus more for the sheet pan

Salt

8 ounces whole wheat penne, small elbow macaroni, or other pasta (about 2 cups)

3 garlic cloves, finely grated or crushed with a garlic press

3 tablespoons chopped Preserved Lemon (page 218)

2 tablespoons fresh lemon juice

2 to 3 tablespoons minced Calabrian chiles

Position racks in the upper and lower thirds of the oven and preheat the oven to 450°F.

Cut the broccoli into ½- to ¾-inch pieces. Lightly brush two heavy large sheet pans with oil. Divide the broccoli between the pans and toss the broccoli on each pan with 2 tablespoons oil. Sprinkle the broccoli very lightly with salt. Roast until tender and browned, about 10 minutes. Cool.

Boil the pasta in a large pot of rapidly boiling salted water until tender but firm to the bite. Drain well and transfer to a large bowl. Immediately add the remaining 2 tablespoons oil and the garlic and toss well. Add the broccoli, preserved lemon, and lemon juice. Add the chiles gradually until spiced to your taste. (The salad can be prepared up to 1 day ahead. Cover and refrigerate.)

loaded orzo

This big, easy salad incorporates all the greatest hits of the Italian market.

Sun-dried tomatoes have fallen out of fashion since their '80s heyday, but after years of avoiding them, I've come to appreciate their concentrated flavor and chewy texture. My favorite sun-dried tomatoes are the still-moist, pliable ones that come in a bag, but any kind is good here. If your sun-dried tomatoes are very dry, soak them briefly in hot water and drain well before using. If marinated or packed in oil, drain those too.

1½ cups (about 10 ounces) orzo

Salt

⅓ cup extra-virgin olive oil

2 garlic cloves, finely grated or crushed with a garlic press

⅓ cup chopped pitted kalamata olives

¼ cup balsamic vinegar

2 tablespoons red wine vinegar

⅓ cup coarsely chopped sun-dried tomatoes

1 pound perlini (tiny fresh mozzarella balls), drained, or other mozzarella, diced

3 cups wild or baby arugula

1 small head radicchio, finely chopped

½ cup chopped fresh basil

½ cup freshly grated Parmesan cheese

½ cup pine nuts, toasted

Freshly grated black pepper

Cook the orzo in a pot of salted water until tender but still firm to the bite. Drain well and transfer to a large bowl. Immediately add the oil and garlic and stir to combine. Mix in the olives and both vinegars and let stand until cooled to room temperature. Stir in the sun-dried tomatoes. *(This can be prepared up to 6 hours ahead. Cover and refrigerate. Bring to room temperature before continuing.)*

Mix in the perlini, arugula, radicchio, basil, Parmesan, and pine nuts. Season the salad with salt and pepper and serve.

ginger-sesame noodles, salad, cashews

4 TO 6 SERVINGS / VEGAN

Noodles, cabbage slaw, and crunchy cashews are tossed in slightly sweet and spicy sesame dressing. Putting the steaming hot spaghetti directly on the slaw lets the heat of the pasta tenderize the vegetables in this Pan Asian–style salad.

Dressing

¼ cup plus 2 tablespoons soy sauce or tamari

¼ cup plus 2 tablespoons Chinese black vinegar or sherry vinegar

⅓ cup toasted sesame oil

⅓ cup tahini

3 tablespoons grated fresh ginger

4 garlic cloves, finely grated or crushed with a garlic press

3 tablespoons brown sugar

1 tablespoon sambal oelek

1 tablespoon fresh lemon or lime juice

Salad

3 cups thinly sliced or shredded green cabbage

3 cups thinly sliced or shredded red cabbage

1 jumbo carrot, trimmed and cut into julienne strips (about 1 cup)

1 red bell pepper, cut into thin strips

12 ounces spaghetti

2 tablespoons toasted sesame oil

6 green onions, thinly sliced

1 cup roasted and salted cashews

½ cup chopped fresh cilantro

¼ cup toasted sesame seeds

For the dressing: Whisk the ingredients to blend in a medium bowl. (*The dressing can be prepared up to 1 week ahead. Cover and refrigerate.*)

For the salad: Combine the green cabbage, red cabbage, carrot, and bell pepper in a large bowl. Cook the noodles in a large pot of rapidly boiling salted water until al dente. Drain well, reserving ¼ cup of the cooking liquid. Immediately add the hot noodles to the cabbage mixture in the bowl. Drizzle the noodles with the toasted sesame oil and toss to combine. Cover and cool completely. Whisk the reserved cooking liquid into the dressing. (*The salad can be made up to 3 hours ahead. Cover and keep at cool room temperature.*)

Just before serving: Add the dressing, green onions, cashews, cilantro, and sesame seeds and toss well.

bread salads

Salads with crunch are great, and toasted bread, in the form of a crouton, crust, crumb, crisp, or point, is the perfect way to achieve that desired texture while adding flavor and heft. The first time I tasted an Italian panzanella salad, the idea of so much bread soaked with ripe tomato juice, garlicky vinegar, and fruity olive oil seemed novel. But I realized that I'd enjoyed eating "bread" salads as a kid in the form of Mom's crouton-topped dinner salad, and that bread-eating cultures have long used bread as an ingredient for salads. Stale bread is inevitable, and for people who make their own bread or for the good people who don't like food going to waste, the crouton is a delicious solution to that problem. While the French may have invented the crouton, Italians have crostini. In Spain, fried breadcrumbs, or *migas*, are enjoyed in many dishes, and Lebanese fattoush is all about crisp bits of flatbread. Large-format croutons in the form of whole-grain toasties complement the richness of egg salad, and as mentioned in the introduction to this book, I have created a very fun salad pizza—a bread lover's delight.

egg salad, ricotta, herbs, sprouted grain toasties

4 SERVINGS

For something as common as egg salad, hard-boiled eggs made creamy and herbaceous can taste downright decadent. I have made lots of egg salad in my life, mostly in spring when my backyard chickens are most productive. Years of tinkering led me to a favorite mix of ricotta and sour cream. The ricotta moistens and lightens the salad without weighing it down (mayo!) or adding too much tang (yogurt!). Mint, tarragon, and chives celebrate spring but can be swapped for green onions or dill. Optional nasturtium flowers add color and a subtle garlic kick. For the best "toasties," look for sprouted whole-grain bread that doesn't list sweeteners in the ingredients.

8 large eggs

4 slices sprouted whole-grain bread

Extra-virgin olive oil, for brushing

¾ teaspoon salt, plus more for sprinkling

⅓ cup whole-milk ricotta cheese

⅓ cup sour cream

1 slightly rounded tablespoon Dijon mustard

1 slightly rounded tablespoon whole-grain Dijon mustard

⅓ cup chopped fresh chives

2 tablespoons chopped fresh mint

2 tablespoons chopped fresh tarragon

6 cups crispy lettuce, such as Salanova

Nasturtium flowers (optional)

Put the eggs in a large saucepan, cover them with water, and bring to a gentle simmer. Simmer for 5 minutes, then remove the eggs from the heat; cover and let stand for 5 minutes. Remove the eggs from the water, then rinse with cold water to cool. Refrigerate until well chilled. *(The eggs can be hard-boiled and stored in the refrigerator for up to 1 week.)*

Stack the bread slices on a cutting board and trim off the crusts. Brush the slices generously with oil, sprinkle with salt, and cut each slice diagonally into quarters, creating 4 triangles per slice. Toast the bread in the oven or a toaster until lightly browned. Cool completely. *(The toasties can be made up to 1 day ahead. Store in an airtight container at room temperature.)*

Stir together the ricotta, sour cream, both mustards, and salt in a medium bowl until well blended. Combine the chives, mint, and tarragon in a small bowl. Peel the eggs. Coarsely chop 4 of the eggs and stir them into the ricotta mixture along with half the herbs. Line a platter or plates with lettuce. Top with the ricotta mixture. Slice the remaining eggs. Arrange the egg slices and toasties atop the salad and sprinkle with the remaining herbs. Garnish with nasturtiums, if desired, and serve.

arugula cacio e pepe pizza

MAKES 4 PIZZAS, 4 TO 6 SERVINGS

Cacio e pepe is a traditional Roman pasta dish. The "sauce" is made by emulsifying generous amounts of grated pecorino into pasta cooking liquid and seasoning the results with a hefty amount of freshly cracked black pepper. The results are boldly satisfying for just a few ingredients. The Roman flavor combo translates well to other foods like salads, breads, and especially pizza.

Cacio e pepe pizza is credited to chef Stefano Callegari, who came up with the technique of putting ice on the pizza dough to keep it moist and chewy in the center. My rendition riffs on his creation—with a fresh topping of cacio e pepe–seasoned arugula. The pizza dough recipe is my own, developed after years of trying various techniques. The dough comes together easily but needs resting time for the best flavor and texture. It should be started two to six days ahead. I use all-purpose flour, not fancy Italian 00 flour, because I like the flavor of the less refined flour. The addition of orange zest comes from a pizziaola who told me the hint of sweet citrus was a secret ingredient in Nancy Silverton's Mozza pizza dough. Perhaps he was pulling my leg, but no matter—it's delicious and a nod to my home state, California.

Pizza Dough

1 teaspoon active dry yeast

2 cups room-temperature water

4¾ cups (641 grams) unbleached all-purpose flour, plus more for dusting

1 tablespoon brown sugar

1½ teaspoons salt

½ teaspoon orange zest (optional)

Extra-virgin olive oil, for drizzling and brushing

Semolina or rice flour, for dusting (if using a pizza oven)

8 tablespoons crushed or broken ice

1¼ cups finely grated Pecorino Romano cheese

Freshly cracked black pepper

8 cups arugula

Sprinkle the yeast over the water in a 2-cup measuring cup and let stand until the yeast dissolves, about 5 minutes.

Fit a heavy-duty mixer with the dough hook. Combine the flour, brown sugar, and salt in the mixer bowl and stir to blend. If using the orange zest, stir it into the yeast mixture. With the mixer running, gradually pour in the yeast mixture. Continue mixing, stopping the machine once or twice to scrape down the sides of the bowl, until the flour and liquid are blended. Increase the speed to high and knead with the hook until a very smooth and sticky dough forms, about 7 minutes. (Yes, 7 minutes!)

Drizzle a 9 x 13-inch baking dish generously with enough oil to coat the bottom of the dish. Using a silicone spatula, transfer the dough to the prepared dish (the dough will be wet). Fold the dough into thirds, like a business letter. Cover with plastic wrap and refrigerate overnight or for up to 2 days, repeating the folding once or twice a day.

Brush four 2-cup-capacity food jars or storage containers with oil. Using a bench knife, large cleaver, or chef's knife, cut the cold dough into 4 even pieces (about 9 ounces each). On a lightly oiled surface, shape each piece into a round. Transfer one dough piece to each jar and seal. Refrigerate the dough overnight or for up to 4 days.

Position racks in the upper and lower thirds of the oven and preheat to 500°F.

Fill a shallow bowl with flour. Dust two heavy large sheet pans lightly with flour. Working with one dough piece at a time, dip the dough round into the bowl of flour to lightly coat. Holding the dough at the top edges with both hands (like a steering wheel), carefully stretch the dough into a 9- to 10-inch round by rotating it and keeping your hands in the same position. Transfer the round to the prepared pan. Repeat with another piece of dough and pan. Brush the pizzas lightly with oil. Scatter 2 tablespoons of the ice over the center of each pizza. Bake until the pizzas are golden brown, 10 to 12 minutes, alternating the baking position about halfway through baking. Immediately sprinkle ¼ cup cheese over each pizza. Season the pizzas very generously with pepper and drizzle with oil. Toss the arugula with enough olive oil to coat and the remaining ¼ cup cheese. Top the pizzas with half the arugula and serve. Repeat with the remaining pizzas and arugula.

Note: This recipe is configured for a standard oven, but it works deliciously in a pizza oven. If using a pizza oven, preheat the oven to 600° to 750°F. Dust a pizza peel instead of a pan with semolina. Slide the pizza off the peel into the oven and bake until golden brown in the center and freckled with dark brown on the edges, 5 to 7 minutes. Finish as instructed.

breaded baked goat cheese, frisée, wild mushrooms, asparagus

4 SERVINGS

I remember eating and loving several iterations of baked goat cheese salad when I was an exchange student in the southwest of France, but the first time I made the dish, I followed Alice Waters's recipe from her seminal *Chez Panisse Menu Cookbook* carefully, to excellent results. Her Baked Goat Cheese with Garden Salad inspired so many chefs that the simple French starter nearly became a California cuisine cliché. I could never tire of warm goat cheese and greens, though, and this version, unlike the original, is chunky with big, crunchy bits of country bread. Sitting on a "nest" of frisée, roasted mushrooms, and asparagus, the Franco-Californian standard transforms into a fine main course.

Goat Cheese

⅓ cup extra-virgin olive oil

1 garlic clove, finely grated or crushed with a garlic press

2 teaspoons fresh thyme leaves, or a pinch of dried thyme, crumbled

6 ounces soft fresh goat cheese log, cut into 4 rounds

8 ounces fresh or day-old country or ciabatta loaf

Dressing

¼ cup extra-virgin olive oil

2½ tablespoons red wine vinegar

2 tablespoons finely chopped shallot

1 teaspoon honey

½ teaspoon Dijon mustard

¼ teaspoon salt

Salad

1 bunch asparagus, well trimmed

4 tablespoons extra-virgin olive oil

12 ounces wild mushrooms, such as oyster, chanterelle, or morel

Salt and freshly ground black pepper

4 cups frisée (torn into bite-sized pieces)

For the goat cheese: Mix the oil, garlic, and thyme in the bottom of a large pie dish. Using your hands, carefully flatten the goat cheese into ½-inch-thick rounds. Place the cheese rounds in the oil and gently turn to coat the cheese with oil.

For the breadcrumbs: Position racks in the top and bottom thirds of the oven and preheat to 400°F.

Trim away the bottom and end crust of the loaf. Using a food processor, pulse the bread until broken into ¼- to ½-inch crumbs. You should have approximately 3 cups. Spread the crumbs evenly over a heavy large sheet pan and lightly toast in the oven for about 5 minutes. If you're working through the rest of the recipe now, increase the oven temperature to 425°F. Transfer the crumbs to a shallow bowl. *(The cheese and crumbs can be prepared ahead. The cheese will keep at cool room temperature for up to 4 hours or can be refrigerated overnight. The crumbs can be prepared up to 1 day ahead and stored in an airtight container at room temperature.)*

For the dressing: Whisk together the ingredients to blend in a small bowl.

For the salad: If you made the breadcrumbs in advance, preheat the oven to 425°F now.

Toss the asparagus with 1 tablespoon of the oil on a heavy large sheet pan. On another heavy large sheet pan, toss the mushrooms with the remaining 3 tablespoons oil. Sprinkle the asparagus and mushrooms lightly with salt and pepper and roast until tender and browned, about 6 minutes.

Press the crumbs into the cheese, flattening the patties slightly and coating them entirely. Toss the remaining crumbs with the excess marinating oil and mound them atop the cheese rounds. Bake until golden brown, about 10 minutes.

Toss the frisée with half the dressing and divide it among plates. Top the frisée with the asparagus and mushrooms and drizzle with additional dressing. Top with the warm goat cheese and serve.

herby fattoush,
sumac-cumin pita crisps

6 TO 8 SERVINGS / VEGAN OPTION

Fattoush is a Lebanese bread salad. It blends crisped sumac-dusted pita, fresh vegetables, a punch of herbs, and garlicky dressing. Purslane is a new green for some—it's a succulent sprout often considered a weed, but the small leaves burst pleasantly with tartness when bitten. Look for purslane at Middle Eastern markets or Mexican markets (where it's called *verdolaga*). This salad is adaptable to the season, and in spring, I add tender fava beans in place of the chickpeas. For salty tang and protein, crumbled feta is a must, but if you're avoiding dairy, sliced olives do the trick. I make my own crunchy pita chips with stale pita for the salad, brushed liberally with fruity olive oil and sprinkled with sumac and cumin—but if you're short on time, simply purchase pita chips to use instead. Sumac and purslane add a lemony punch to the fattoush, but the salad is good and authentic served with an extra lemon wedge instead.

1 (14- to 16-ounce) can chickpeas, rinsed and drained, or 1½ cups cooked and cooled fresh or frozen double-peeled fava beans

½ red onion, cut in half lengthwise and thinly sliced

Lemony Dressing (recipe follows)

6 cups mixed greens, such as baby kale, wild arugula, torn dandelion greens, watercress, and sliced romaine

1 bunch radishes, trimmed and sliced

2 Persian or pickling cucumbers, sliced

1 cup purslane leaves (from about 2 bunches; optional)

1 cup mixed fresh herbs, such as mint, cilantro, Italian parsley, and dill

1 cup very thinly sliced red cabbage

4 to 6 cups Sumac-Cumin Pita Crisps (recipe follows)

6 ounces feta cheese, crumbled (optional)

3 small ripe tomatoes, cut into wedges, or about 1½ cups cherry tomatoes, cut in half

Combine the chickpeas and onions in a large bowl. Add ⅓ cup of the dressing and let stand while you prepare the rest of the salad.

Add the greens, radishes, cucumbers, purslane, herbs, and cabbage to the bean mixture in the bowl. Add the pita crisps, cheese, if desired, and tomatoes. Add more dressing to taste, toss well, and serve.

recipe continues

sumac-cumin pita crisps

Sumac is a spice made from the ground berries of the sumac bush. It has a tart-sweet flavor. Find sumac at Middle Eastern markets and online at Penzeys.

4 (6-inch) or 3 (11-inch) pita breads

Extra-virgin olive oil, for brushing and drizzling

1 tablespoon ground sumac, plus more for sprinkling

1 tablespoon ground cumin, plus more for sprinkling

Salt

Aleppo pepper

Preheat the oven to 350°F.

Brush both sides of the pita breads with oil. Stack the rounds and cut them into approximately 1½-inch squares. Transfer the pita squares to a large bowl. Drizzle generously with additional oil and toss until the pieces are well coated. Sprinkle with the sumac and cumin and toss well. Spread the pita pieces out on a heavy large sheet pan and sprinkle generously with additional sumac and cumin, and some salt and Aleppo pepper. Bake until crisp and golden brown, stirring once or twice, about 7 minutes. Remove from the oven and let cool. *(The pita chips can be prepared up to 4 days ahead. Store them in an airtight container at room temperature.)*

lemony dressing

MAKES ABOUT 1¾ CUPS

This dressing is excellent when drizzled over grilled or steamed vegetables or spread on eggplant sandwiches.

3 tablespoons tahini

2 garlic cloves, finely grated or crushed with a garlic press

1 generous teaspoon salt

½ cup fresh lemon juice

1 cup extra-virgin olive oil

1 tablespoon ground sumac

Combine the tahini, garlic, and salt in a medium bowl. Gradually whisk in the lemon juice, then the oil and sumac. *(The dressing can be made 1 week ahead. Cover and refrigerate.)*

chopped salad, migas, spanish goodies

4 SERVINGS

Migas are a Spanish version of croutons made from large breadcrumbs that are sautéed in olive oil until golden and crisp. Migas are often served with soups and egg dishes, but here they add crunch to a chopped salad that's influenced by the flavors of Spain. Stir-frying the chickpeas with smoked paprika, garlic, and sherry wine vinegar instantly transforms them into tasty chorizo-like bits.

Migas

2 garlic cloves, finely grated or crushed with a garlic press

3 cups coarse fresh sourdough or country white breadcrumbs (¼- to ½-inch pieces)

¼ cup extra-virgin olive oil

Salt and freshly ground black pepper

Chickpeas

1 (14- to 16-ounce) can chickpeas, rinsed and drained

1 tablespoon extra-virgin olive oil

1 garlic clove, finely grated or crushed with a garlic press

2 teaspoons smoked paprika

1 tablespoon sherry wine vinegar

1 teaspoon finely chopped fresh oregano or ½ teaspoon dried oregano, crumbled

Dressing

⅓ cup extra-virgin olive oil

2 tablespoons sherry wine vinegar

1½ teaspoons honey

½ teaspoon salt

½ teaspoon orange zest

Salad

8 cups mixed greens, such as romaine, arugula, frisée, and spinach

2 small tart green apples, cored and sliced into strips

1 (6-ounce) wedge Manchego cheese, diced (about 1¼ cups)

1 red bell pepper, diced, or 6 mini bell peppers, sliced

½ cup chopped sweet onion

⅔ cup chopped roasted Marcona or other roasted almonds

For the migas: Massage the garlic into the bread. Heat the oil in a heavy large skillet over medium heat. Add the bread and stir with a wooden spoon to coat with oil. Sprinkle the migas with salt and pepper and sauté until golden brown and chewy-crisp, about 8 minutes. Transfer the migas to a bowl and cool completely. (The migas can be made up to 1 day ahead. Store at room temperature in an airtight container.)

For the chickpeas: Place the drained chickpeas in the center of a clean kitchen towel. Enclose the chickpeas in the towel and rub gently, both drying and slipping off the translucent jackets.

recipe continues

In the same skillet (no need to wash), heat the oil over medium-high heat. Add the chickpeas and stir until just beginning to pop, about 1 minute. Add the garlic and paprika and stir until fragrant. Pour the vinegar over the chickpeas, sprinkle with the oregano, and stir until the vinegar evaporates and the chickpeas are tender and nicely coated, about 1 minute. Cool and season with salt.

For the dressing: In a small bowl, whisk the oil, vinegar, honey, salt, and orange zest to blend.

For the salad: Combine the greens, apple, cheese, red pepper, and onion in a large bowl. Toss the salad with half of the dressing. Sprinkle the salad with the chickpeas, migas, and almonds. Drizzle with the remaining dressing and serve.

Tip: You can make fresh crumbs quickly by pulsing 2-inch pieces of bread in the food processor until crumbled into ¼- to ½-inch bits.

SALAD PARTY

While this book isn't specifically about entertaining, it can serve as inspiration and a guide for hosting a salad party. Many of the recipes combine well with others, as they share similar influences or seasonality. I've fed guests with a mix of salad offerings: Arroz con Cosas (Paella-Style Salad, page 84) with Chopped Salad, Migas, Spanish Goodies (page 175) and Dandelion Greens, Roasted Potatoes, Romesco (page 195) for a dinner with Spanish flavors; and Carrot, Bulgur, Green Olives, Arugula, Date, Preserved Lemon (page 58) with Muhammara, Turnip, Pomegranate, Dandelion Green Slaw, Walnuts (page 92); Herby Fattoush, Sumac-Cumin Pita Crisps (page 173); and Chickpeas, Cauliflower, Tomato, Sumac Yogurt (page 188) for a dinner influenced by the flavors of the Middle East. To create your own salad menu, you don't have to stick to a geographical region; just be sure that you don't overlap too many of the same flavors or ingredients. A party featuring Beet Hummus, Fioretto, Pine Nut Gremolata (page 97); Lettuce Cups, Thai Flavors, Cauliflower Tempeh (page 48); Coconut Quinoa, Black Beans, Avocado, Mango, Collards, Plantain, Cashews (page 129); and Roasted Whole Butternut Squash, Salsa Macha, Kale, Cotija Cheese (page 196) spotlights flavors from many different cultures but still presents compatible flavors without relying too heavily on a particular grain, pulse, or seed. The serving sizes for the recipes in this book range from two to about eight servings, but when hosting a salad party, remember that recipes that serve two as a main course make great appetizers when feeding larger groups. Because the majority of the salads can be prepared ahead and transport well, they'd also make for a fun "assigned recipe" potluck, or "bowl-luck."

broccoli salad with olive, pecorino, lemon, croutons

2 TO 4 SERVINGS

Lightly steamed tender florets and crunchy raw sticks cut from broccoli stalks combine with tart lemon, salty olives, and rich egg and cheese in this Italian-inspired, crouton-topped salad. I like to add plenty of the toasted bread bits to my serving, but feel free to add as many or few as you like.

⅓ cup extra-virgin olive oil

1 large garlic clove, finely grated or crushed with a garlic press

1 large bunch broccoli (about 1½ pounds)

Salt

3 tablespoons red wine vinegar

½ teaspoon grated lemon zest

¼ teaspoon red pepper flakes

⅓ cup oil-cured black olives, pitted and chopped

½ cup thinly sliced red onion

½ cup coarsely grated Pecorino Romano cheese

2 hard-boiled eggs, peeled and chopped

Rustic Croutons (page 219)

Lemon wedges, for garnish

Whisk together the oil and garlic to blend in a small bowl.

Cut the flowering tops from the broccoli stalks and trim the tops into ¾-inch florets with 1- to 2-inch-long stems. Bring 1 inch of water to a boil in a heavy large skillet. Add a generous sprinkle of salt. Add the florets, cover, and cook until just crisp-tender, about 3 minutes. Drain well and transfer to a large bowl. Drizzle with 2 tablespoons of the oil-garlic mixture and cool.

Peel the broccoli stalks and cut them into sturdy matchstick-sized pieces. Add the broccoli stalks to the florets.

Whisk the vinegar, lemon zest, and red pepper flakes into the remaining oil-garlic mixture and pour this mixture over the broccoli. Add the olives, onion, and cheese and toss well. Spoon the salad onto plates and top with the hard-boiled eggs and croutons. Garnish with lemon wedges and serve.

summer panzanella, burrata, pesto drizzle

SERVES 4 TO 6

Panzanella is a traditional Italian salad made with bread and tomatoes. The key to transforming these simple ingredients into an amazing dish is using super-ripe tomatoes and good bread. I like to use the croutons made from my own naturally leavened bread, which I always have in the freezer, but whole wheat levain, country loaf, or other bread with a good crust such as pain rustique or ciabatta will work. This version of panzanella gets elevated with the additions of rich burrata and drops of jade-green pesto drizzle. If you don't have the time or inclination to make the drizzle, you can simply toss in a generous handful of fresh basil leaves.

2 pounds assorted ripe heirloom tomatoes, cut into wedges

1 large Persian cucumber, 2 pickling cucumbers, or ½ hothouse cucumber, cut in half lengthwise and thinly sliced

½ small red onion, very thinly sliced

¼ cup wild capers, preferably salt-packed

2 garlic cloves, finely grated or crushed with a garlic press

½ teaspoon salt

¼ cup plus 2 tablespoons extra-virgin olive oil

3 to 4 tablespoons red wine vinegar

4 cups (about 7.5 ounces) 1-inch rustic bread pieces

¾ cup freshly grated Parmesan cheese

¼ cup fresh basil leaves, torn into pieces

Freshly ground black pepper

8 ounces burrata cheese, each ball cut in half

Pesto Drizzle (page 216)

2 to 4 cups wild arugula

Combine the tomatoes, cucumber, onion, capers, garlic, and salt in a large bowl. Gently stir in ¼ cup of the oil and 3 tablespoons of the vinegar and let stand until the tomatoes become very juicy, about 20 minutes, or for up to 4 hours.

Meanwhile, preheat the oven or a toaster oven to 400°F.

Toss the bread pieces with the remaining 2 tablespoons oil and a little salt on a heavy small sheet pan and toast the bread in the oven until golden brown, about 5 minutes.

Toss the bread into the salad and let stand until the bread softens slightly with the tomato juices, about 10 minutes. Gently mix in the Parmesan and basil. Season the salad with pepper, the remaining 1 tablespoon vinegar, and additional salt, if necessary. Transfer the salad to a large deep platter. Top with the burrata. Spoon some pesto drizzle over the burrata, scatter the arugula on top, and serve.

Note: If keeping cubes of bread in your freezer is not your thing, simply cut about 6 ounces (a little less than half a 1-pound loaf) into thick slices. Brush the slices with olive oil, lightly toast, and tear the toasted slices into 1-inch pieces—easy!

fall bread salad

4 SERVINGS / VEGAN OPTION

Loaded with fall produce, this warm salad makes a great alternative to Thanksgiving stuffing. Nice bits of aged Gouda, blue cheese, or gooey Camembert can be added to the mix to make it indulgent.

4 cups (¾-inch) pieces country or rustic bread (from about one-third of a 1-pound loaf)

6 tablespoons extra-virgin olive oil

3 garlic cloves, minced, finely grated, or crushed with a garlic press

3 teaspoons chopped fresh thyme leaves

Salt

4 cups (¾- to 1-inch) diced, peeled butternut squash (from about one 1¼-pound squash)

12 ounces golden and/or Chioggia (candy cane) beets (about 2 medium), trimmed, peeled, and cut into ½-inch-thick wedges

Freshly ground black pepper

1 cup vegetable broth

2 to 3 tablespoons white wine vinegar

1 tablespoon honey or maple syrup

½ cup dry white wine

8 cups wintery greens, such as red mustard, baby kale, kale, chard, escarole, mizuna, and radicchio, torn into 4-inch pieces if large

2 small firm ripe pears, cored and sliced

¼ small red onion, very thinly sliced

½ cup chopped dried cranberries

½ cup toasted pecans, walnuts, or hazelnuts

Preheat the oven to 350°F.

Toss the bread pieces in a large bowl with 2 tablespoons of the oil, one-third of the garlic, 1 teaspoon of the thyme, and a sprinkle of salt. Spread the bread out on a heavy sheet pan. Bake until lightly toasted, about 10 minutes. Return the toasted bread pieces to the same large bowl.

Increase the oven temperature to 425°F.

Toss the squash and beets with 2 tablespoons of the oil, the rest of the garlic, and remaining 2 teaspoons thyme on a heavy large sheet pan. Season with salt and pepper and roast until softened and browned, stirring twice, about 35 minutes.

Meanwhile, boil the broth in a small saucepan over high heat until reduced to ¼ cup, about 12 minutes. Remove from the heat and stir in the remaining 2 tablespoons oil, 2 tablespoons vinegar, and the honey.

Transfer the hot squash and beets to the bowl with the bread. Add the wine to the sheet pan and stir over medium-high heat, boiling and stirring up the browned bits from the bottom of the pan until the liquid has reduced by half, about 3 minutes. Add the reduction to the broth mixture; bring it to a simmer and pour it over the bread mixture. Add the greens, pears, red onion, cranberries, and pecans and toss well. Season with pepper and additional vinegar, if desired, and serve.

spring panzanella, creamy pecorino dressing

4 SERVINGS

In this panzanella, I use freshly pulled croutons as opposed to my stash of frozen homemade bread cubes. Using a Nancy Silverton technique from her *Breads from the La Brea Bakery* cookbook, I "pull" the bread into roughly shaped pieces—pieces that get delightfully coated with creamy dressing.

Dressing

1 cup freshly grated Pecorino Romano cheese

½ cup buttermilk

⅓ cup extra-virgin olive oil

1 green onion, cut into 2-inch pieces

1 garlic clove, peeled

¼ teaspoon salt

2 to 3 tablespoons fresh lemon juice

Freshly ground black pepper

Croutons

8 ounces fresh country bread

3 tablespoons extra-virgin olive oil

Salt

Salad

1 bunch asparagus (about 14 ounces)

8 cups mixed spring salad greens, such as arugula and Bibb lettuce

1 hothouse cucumber, halved lengthwise and sliced

4 ounces sugar snap peas, thinly sliced on a long diagonal

8 radishes, thinly sliced

8 ounces (or more) small fresh mozzarella cheese balls, thinly sliced

2 ounces Pecorino Romano cheese, shaved, for garnish

For the dressing: Blend the Pecorino Romano, buttermilk, oil, green onion, garlic, and salt in a blender until smooth. Add the lemon juice to taste and season with pepper. *(The dressing can be made up to 4 days ahead; cover and refrigerate.)*

For the croutons: Preheat the oven to 400°F.

Gently pull the bread apart, creating roughly shaped ¾-inch pieces. (You should have about 4 cups.) Toss the croutons with the oil on a heavy medium sheet pan. Sprinkle lightly with salt and toast in the oven until golden brown, about 5 minutes. Cool. *(The croutons can be made up to 1 day ahead. Cover and keep at room temperature.)*

For the salad: Working with one at a time, grasp an asparagus stalk firmly at the cut end. Using a sharp vegetable peeler, shave the asparagus into thin ribbons; discard the tough end. Repeat with the remaining spears. (Don't worry if the tips break off or if some pieces are thicker than others.) Transfer the asparagus to a large bowl. Add the greens, cucumber, snap peas, and radishes. *(This can be prepared up to 3 hours before serving.)*

When ready to serve: Add the mozzarella, croutons, and dressing. Season generously with pepper, toss well, and serve garnished with the Pecorino Romano.

roasted & toasted salads

These salads in part or in their entirety come out hot and toasty from the oven or crispy brown from a sizzling skillet. Roasting vegetables at high heat concentrates their flavor, and the resulting caramelized bits bring a taste bonus to any dish, especially salads. A whole roasted vegetable, like a head of cauliflower or quartered butternut squash, makes for an impressive centerpiece to dinner, a focal point for a salad that won't make a vegetarian feel slighted or somehow relegated to yet another uninspired steamed-veggie plate. When potatoes or slices of squash are roasted to tender, toasty, and golden brown, they only need a spoonful of aromatic charmoula condiment or a punchy romesco sauce along with a requisite handful of spicy greens to taste elevated. Indeed, all the recipes in this chapter have a festive quality to them—the sharing of colorful baked pepperonata, the sprinkling of fragrant dukkah over roasted feta and lemons, or just the magic of a chickpea pancake or the fun of fried tempeh. These salads are ready for a toast.

chickpeas, cauliflower, tomato, sumac yogurt

4 SERVINGS / GF

This salad highlights the technique of oven-roasting at high temperature. The flavors of the cauliflower and cherry tomatoes develop and become concentrated while the chickpeas get nicely crisped. Cool yogurt with a zing of garlic rounds out the trio, while the sumac lends its fruity-tart and tannic zest. This dinner can be made ahead so it can be ready after a busy day.

1½ cups plain Greek yogurt

1 garlic clove, finely grated or crushed with a garlic press

1 generous teaspoon ground sumac, plus more for sprinkling

5 tablespoons extra-virgin olive oil, plus more for brushing

1 large head cauliflower, cut into 2-inch florets

Salt and freshly ground black pepper

12 ounces cherry tomatoes or other small tomatoes (about 2 cups)

1 (14- to 16-ounce) can chickpeas, rinsed and drained

1 rounded teaspoon cumin seeds

1 teaspoon Aleppo pepper

½ cup chopped fresh Italian parsley

Stir together the yogurt, garlic, and sumac to blend in a small bowl. (*The yogurt can be made ahead and refrigerated for up to 4 days.*)

Preheat the oven to 425°F.

Brush two heavy large sheet pans with oil. Toss the cauliflower with 3 tablespoons of the oil on one prepared sheet pan. Spread the cauliflower out into a single layer and season with salt and pepper. Toss the tomatoes with 1 tablespoon of the oil on the second prepared sheet pan and season with salt and pepper. Roast the cauliflower until tender and well browned and the tomatoes until blistered in spots, stirring once, about 30 minutes. Transfer the tomatoes to a plate to cool. Add the chickpeas and the remaining 1 tablespoon oil to the same pan and toss to coat. Sprinkle the chickpeas with the cumin seeds and Aleppo pepper and roast until lightly browned and fragrant, about 10 minutes. Cool completely. Combine the cauliflower, tomatoes, chickpeas, and parsley in a large bowl and toss carefully just to blend. (*The salad can be prepared ahead. Keep at cool room temperature for up to 6 hours or refrigerate overnight. Allow to warm to room temperature before serving.*)

Spoon the yogurt onto a plate or shallow bowl and surround with the salad. Sprinkle generously with sumac and serve.

whole roasted cauliflower
with mung beans, greens, and black tahini

2 SERVINGS / GF, VEGAN

A head of roasted cauliflower is so deliciously and visually substantial that it seems almost celebratory, in the same way that a whole roast chicken does. No wonder cooks and chefs have turned roasting cauliflower to dark brown, crisp, and meltingly tender into a "thing." I serve the cauliflower in all its glory atop a mung bean salad with a drizzle of striking black tahini. Black tahini is sweeter and more complex in flavor than the golden-hued variety, but if you can't find it, go ahead and use a small amount of the regular kind. Mung beans are very popular in India, where they are simmered up into dal, or sprouted. They are small and green and very nutritious, but the salad is also very nice with lentils.

½ cup dried mung beans, soaked overnight and drained, or 1 cup cooked lentils

¼ teaspoon salt, plus more for sprinkling

2 small cauliflower heads (about 1 pound each), or 1 larger head, cut in half

6 tablespoons extra-virgin olive oil

3 tablespoons fresh lemon juice

1 garlic clove, finely grated or crushed with a garlic press

6 pitted dates, sliced

1 green onion, white and pale green parts separated from the green parts, very thinly sliced

Freshly ground black pepper

3 cups baby lettuce greens

Black tahini, for drizzling

Combine the mung beans and enough cool water to cover by a few inches in a heavy large saucepan and bring to a boil over high heat. Reduce the heat to medium-low and simmer until the beans begin to become tender, about 10 minutes. Add a generous pinch of salt and simmer until the beans are very tender but still retain their shape, about 10 minutes longer. Drain, transfer to a medium bowl, and cool completely. (The mung beans can be made up to 4 days ahead. Cover and refrigerate.)

Preheat the oven to 400°F.

Using a sharp knife, trim away the bottom and tough stem of each cauliflower head. Place the heads in a baking dish. Rub the entire surface of the heads with 3 tablespoons of the oil and sprinkle generously with salt. Cover with foil and bake until just beginning to become tender, about 20 minutes. Uncover and bake until well browned and tender, about 40 minutes more.

Mix the remaining 3 tablespoons oil, the lemon juice, garlic, and ¼ teaspoon salt in a small bowl. Add ¼ cup of the dressing to the mung beans. Add the dates and the white and pale green parts of the green onions and season with salt and pepper. Gently toss the lettuce with the remaining dressing and season with salt and pepper. Divide the lettuce and mung beans between two salad bowls. Carefully place a cauliflower in the center of each salad. Drizzle with tahini, sprinkle with the green parts of the green onions, and serve.

salade "gratinée" with roasted fingerlings, red onions

2 SERVINGS / GF

Sheet pan dinners are easy to assemble, and the cleanup is quick, as you tend to dirty just one pan. The French word *gratinée* refers to something capped with melted, toasted cheese. Combining the simplicity of a sheet pan dinner with broiled cheese is a cheese lover's dream on a cozy winter evening. Be sure to use sturdy greens when making this warm salad.

2 tablespoons extra-virgin olive oil, plus more for brushing

12 ounces fingerling potatoes, cut in half lengthwise

Salt and freshly ground black pepper

1 small red onion, cut into 16 wedges

½ lemon, halved lengthwise and thinly sliced

6 cups packed mixed robust greens, such as kale, dandelion, radicchio, and escarole

1 tablespoon red wine vinegar

1 cup grated aged Gruyère cheese

Preheat the oven to 450°F.

Brush a heavy large sheet pan with oil. Toss the potatoes with 1 tablespoon of the oil on the sheet pan. Season with salt and pepper and roast until golden brown and just tender, about 14 minutes. Stir the potatoes, then add the red onion and lemon to the sheet pan. Roast until the potatoes are very tender and the onion and lemon pieces are well browned, about 6 minutes longer.

Switch the oven to broil.

Toss the greens with remaining 1 tablespoon oil, the vinegar, a pinch of salt, and a generous grinding pepper in a large bowl. Spoon the greens evenly over the roasted vegetables on the sheet pan. Sprinkle evenly with the cheese and broil until the cheese melts. Divide the salad between two plates and serve immediately.

dandelion greens,
roasted potatoes, romesco

4 SERVINGS / GF, VEGAN

Warm crispy-tender potatoes and chilled hearty greens come together nicely when napped in robust, garlicky red pepper romesco. It's a speedy dairy-free dinner that's perfect for a weeknight, as you can make the sauce ahead. Elevate workweek nights by beginning your meal with olives, Manchego cheese, and Spanish olive oil crackers.

2 pounds peewee gold or medium Yukon Gold potatoes

3 tablespoons extra-virgin olive oil

Salt and freshly ground black pepper

1 bunch trimmed dandelion greens (about 8 cups)

2 tablespoons sherry vinegar or red wine vinegar

Romesco Sauce (page 216)

2 green onions, thinly sliced (optional)

Preheat the oven to 425°F.

If using peewee potatoes, cut them in half. If using larger potatoes, cut them into ¾- to 1-inch pieces. Brush a heavy large sheet pan with oil. Toss the potatoes with 2 tablespoons of the oil and sprinkle with salt and pepper. Roast the potatoes until tender when pierced with a fork and golden brown, stirring once or twice, about 20 minutes.

Meanwhile, gently massage the greens with the remaining 1 tablespoon oil in a large bowl. Add the vinegar and a sprinkle of salt; toss well. Arrange the greens on a platter or plates and top with the warm potatoes. Spoon some romesco sauce over the salad, sprinkle with the green onions, if desired, and serve.

roasted whole butternut squash, salsa macha, kale, cotija cheese

4 TO 6 SERVING GF

This salad stands alone as a satisfying and complex-flavored dinner, but served with tortillas and slow-simmered black beans, it becomes the centerpiece to a Mexican-influenced vegetarian feast. Roasted at high heat, the squash browns and becomes tender quickly; if you bake bread, this is a perfect way to take advantage of your hot oven.

Squash

1 large butternut squash, (about 2½ pounds), cut lengthwise into quarters and seeded

Extra-virgin olive oil, for brushing

Salt

4 garlic cloves, peeled

Salad

8 cups torn trimmed kale leaves (preferably lacinato)

2 tablespoons extra-virgin olive oil

About 2 tablespoons red wine vinegar

6 to 8 tablespoons finely grated or crumbled Cotija cheese

½ cup pomegranate seeds (optional)

Salsa Macha (page 215)

Edible flower petals, such as marigold and dianthus (optional)

For the squash: Preheat the oven to 450°F.

Brush a heavy large roasting pan lightly with oil. Place the squash pieces cut-side up on the roasting pan, brush lightly with oil, and sprinkle with salt. Place the garlic cloves in the cavity and roast the squash until tender and well browned, about 45 minutes.

For the salad: While the squash is in the oven, combine the kale and oil in a large bowl. Using your hands, gently massage the kale until it softens. Add the vinegar to taste. Toss with enough cheese to your liking. Top the kale with the squash and sprinkle with the pomegranate seeds, if desired. Drizzle generously with salsa macha, sprinkle with flower petals, if desired, and serve.

roasted delicata, goat cheese, arugula, almond charmoula

2 SERVINGS / GF

Charmoula is a Moroccan herb and spice paste that's commonly spread on chicken and fish. With the addition of almonds and extra-virgin olive oil, it becomes a lively topping for vegetables. Delicata squash is small and sweet and the skin cooks up tender, so there is no need to peel it, but butternut squash makes a good substitute.

Charmoula

1 tablespoon cumin seeds

⅔ cup chopped toasted almonds

2 green onions, thinly sliced

⅓ cup coarsely chopped fresh cilantro

⅓ cup coarsely chopped fresh Italian parsley

½ cup extra-virgin olive oil

1 garlic clove, finely grated or crushed with a garlic press

2 teaspoons paprika

½ teaspoon salt

½ teaspoon ground turmeric

Pinch of ground cinnamon

Salad

1 tablespoon extra-virgin olive oil, plus more for brushing

2 delicata squash, cut into ½-inch-thick slices and seeded, or 1 small butternut squash (about 1½ pounds), peeled, halved, seeded, and cut into ½-inch-thick slices

Ras el hanout

Salt

4 cups arugula

4 ounces soft fresh goat cheese

For the charmoula: Stir the cumin seeds in a heavy small saucepan over medium heat until lightly browned and fragrant. Cool the cumin seeds and transfer to a mortar and pestle. Coarsely grind the cumin seeds, then transfer to a medium bowl. Add the remaining ingredients and stir to blend. *(The charmoula can be made up to 1 week ahead. Store in a jar in the refrigerator. Allow to stand at room temperature for 1 hour before serving.)*

For the salad: Preheat the oven to 400°F. Brush a heavy large sheet pan with oil.

Toss the squash with the oil on the pan and arrange in a single layer. Sprinkle the squash with ras el hanout and salt. Roast until golden brown on the bottom, about 15 minutes. Turn the slices and roast until golden brown on both sides and tender, about 5 minutes longer. Cool. *(The squash can be made ahead. Cover and refrigerate for up to 2 days. Allow to stand at room temperature for 1 hour before serving.)*

Divide the arugula between two shallow bowls or plates. Arrange the squash slices atop the arugula and scatter with the goat cheese. Spoon a little charmoula over the salads and serve.

roasted asparagus, broccolini, feta, meyer lemon, green garlic, arugula, pistachio dukkah

2 TO 4 SERVINGS / GF

This spring salad is a layering of textures and temperatures. Asparagus and Broccolini are roasted at high heat with lemon, feta, and springy green garlic. The warm combo gets topped with a scattering of arugula and a sprinkling of dukkah, a nut-spice condiment from Egypt. Be sure to have fresh crusty bread on hand to help scoop up all this flavor.

Dukkah

1 tablespoon coriander seeds

1 tablespoon cumin seeds

1½ teaspoons fennel seeds

⅓ cup shelled pistachios, toasted

2 tablespoons toasted sesame seeds

1 teaspoon Aleppo pepper

½ teaspoon salt

Salad

1 bunch asparagus (about 1 pound), trimmed

1 bunch Broccolini (about 8 ounces), trimmed

1 lemon, preferably Meyer, sliced

⅓ cup sliced green garlic, or 3 garlic cloves, thinly sliced

¼ cup extra-virgin olive oil, plus more for drizzling

8 ounces feta cheese, cut into ½- to ¾-inch-thick slices

Salt and freshly ground black pepper

2 cups arugula

For the dukkah: Stir the coriander, cumin, and fennel seeds together in a heavy small saucepan over medium-high heat until toasted and fragrant. Cool. Transfer the spices to a mortar and pestle or a spice grinder and coarsely grind. Add the pistachios, sesame seeds, Aleppo pepper, and salt and grind until the pistachios are broken into small pieces. *(The dukkah can be made 4 days ahead. Store in a jar at room temperature.)*

For the salad: Preheat the oven to 450°F.

Gently toss the asparagus, Broccolini, lemon, and garlic with the oil on a heavy large sheet pan. Nestle the feta in and among the vegetables and drizzle with a little additional oil. Sprinkle lightly with salt and black pepper. Roast the vegetable mixture in the oven until the vegetables are tender and browned, about 10 minutes. Cool until warm. Scatter the arugula over the sheet pan and drizzle lightly with oil. Sprinkle with the dukkah and serve.

tempeh, spinach, peanutty lime dressing

2 SERVINGS / GF, VEGAN

Tempeh is a traditional Indonesian staple. To make tempeh, partially cooked and husked soybeans are blended with indigenous fungus, shaped into cakes, and fermented. The results are higher in protein, fiber, and vitamins than tofu. I first tasted tempeh at a food stall on Java. Served warm and tossed with crushed peanuts and water spinach, the dish was so good that when I returned home, I tried to re-create it. From *Cradle of Flavor*, James Oseland's book about the food and cooking of Indonesia, Malaysia, and Singapore, I learned that the secret to making flavorful tempeh is to pre-soak it in garlic-infused water before deep-frying it. Water spinach, sometimes called water morning glory because of the shape of its leaves, is prized throughout Southeast Asia. I use hardier and easier-to-find baby spinach for this Java-inspired salad.

Tempeh

1½ cups water

5 garlic cloves, finely grated or crushed with a garlic press

1½ teaspoons salt

1 (8-ounce) package tempeh

Dressing

⅓ cup peanut oil

3 tablespoons fresh lime juice

1 rounded tablespoon natural peanut butter, preferably creamy

1½ tablespoons brown sugar

1½ teaspoons sambal oelek

½ teaspoon salt

Salad

Peanut oil, for frying

8 cups tender spinach leaves

1 green onion, thinly sliced

For the tempeh: Stir together the water, garlic, and salt in a medium bowl to blend. Place the brick of tempeh on a cutting board. Using a small, sharp knife, score the tempeh with shallow cuts, about ¼ inch apart and ⅛ inch deep, forming a grid pattern. Cut the tempeh into approximately 1-inch squares. Using a sharp knife, split the squares in half, creating two squares. Add the tempeh to the garlic water and soak for 30 minutes.

For the dressing: Whisk together the ingredients in a salad bowl to blend.

For the salad: Drain the tempeh and blot dry. Heat 1 inch of oil in a heavy medium skillet over medium-high heat. The oil is ready when a small piece of tempeh sizzles rapidly when added to the pan. Working in batches, fry the tempeh, moving it and turning it in the oil, until golden brown and crisp, about 2 minutes per batch. Drain on paper towels.

　　Add the spinach to the dressing in the bowl, then add the tempeh and toss to coat. Divide the salad between two plates, top with the green onion, and serve.

Tip: If grating or pressing five garlic cloves seems like a chore, you can simply combine the water, salt, and garlic cloves in a blender and whir until the garlic is pureed.

roasted beets, citrus, labneh, zhoug

2 SERVINGS / GF

The jalapeño and cumin in the zhoug bring out the sweet earthy flavor of the beets, and the cardamom plays well with the citrus in this light and simple meal. Wrapping the beets separately to roast might seem like a bother, but a foil jacket helps the beets cook evenly and keeps their color brighter. If I happen to hit the farmers' market just before making this salad, I'll pick up a few cilantro sprouts from the sprout man to add another herbal pop. Serve with warm pita bread and a handful of spicy greens to complete the meal.

1 bunch baby red beets (four or five 2-inch beets)

1 bunch baby golden beets

1 bunch baby Chioggia (candy cane) beets

Extra-virgin olive oil

1 cup labneh

2 generous cups sliced peeled mixed citrus, such as small blood oranges, Cara Cara oranges, and tangerines

Zhoug (page 214)

Cilantro sprouts (optional)

Preheat the oven to 375°F.

Trim and scrub all the beets. Arrange the red beets in the center of a sheet of foil. Drizzle the beets with a small amount of oil and enclose in the foil. Repeat drizzling and wrapping with the golden beets, then the Chioggia beets. Place the beet packets on a shallow pan and roast until tender, about 45 minutes. Cool. *(The beets can be prepared up to 3 days ahead; refrigerate until ready to use.)* Peel and quarter the beets.

Stir the labneh until smooth. Spoon ½ cup of the labneh onto each of two plates. Surround the labneh with the beets and citrus. Drizzle with zhoug, garnish with cilantro sprouts, if desired, and serve.

Swap: Exchange the baby beets for a bunch of larger red beets. If you're really looking to streamline cooking time, Trader Joe's markets and some Middle Eastern restaurants sell versions of zhoug.

baked ricotta pepperonata, herb salad

4 SERVINGS / GF

Cooked salads are an Italian tradition. The salads are cooked during the cool hours of the day and served at room temperature later for lunch or dinner. Classic Italian pepperonata is made of sautéed peppers, onions, and herbs. In this version, I use sweet mini peppers and bake them until tender along with whole-milk ricotta. Top the summery ensemble with arugula, herbs, and a drizzle of good balsamic vinegar. Serve it with warm focaccia or crusty bread.

15 to 16 ounces whole-milk ricotta cheese

2 pounds mini sweet bell peppers, stem ends trimmed

10 ounces grape or cherry tomatoes (about 2 cups)

½ medium red onion, cut into ½-inch-thick slices

16 pitted kalamata olives

6 garlic cloves, chopped

3 tablespoons extra-virgin olive oil, plus more for drizzling

2 tablespoons fresh oregano leaves

½ teaspoon red pepper flakes

½ teaspoon salt

Freshly cracked black pepper

Balsamic vinegar

1 cup arugula leaves

½ cup fresh basil leaves

Line a strainer with cheesecloth and set the strainer over a bowl. Carefully unmold the ricotta into the prepared strainer, retaining the shape of the cheese. Refrigerate the cheese, uncovered, for at least 6 hours or overnight.

Preheat the oven to 425°F.

Cut any peppers larger than your thumb in half. Toss the bell peppers, tomatoes, onion, olives, and garlic with 3 tablespoons of the oil in a 9 x 13-inch baking dish or similar-sized pan. Make a space near the center of the pan. Carefully place the ricotta in the space and drizzle with oil. Sprinkle the bell pepper mixture and cheese with the oregano, red pepper flakes, and salt and season with black pepper. Bake until the cheese and bell peppers are browned and the peppers are tender, about 30 minutes. Cool until warm.

Just before serving, drizzle the pepperonata with vinegar and top with the arugula and basil.

north african-style chickpea pancake, salad turnips, greens, harissa

2 SERVINGS / GF, VEGAN OPTION

Chickpea pancakes are magic. The combination of just chickpea flour and water pan-fries into flannel-like goodness. Versions of chickpea pancakes are popular in Provence, Italy, Spain, North Africa, and Argentina. Bittersweet additions of caramelized onions and dandelion greens and cool-crisp salad turnips complete this North African rendition. In North Africa, the pancakes are traditionally served with a dusting of ground cumin and a spoonful of harissa, the spicy red pepper condiment of the region. Harissa adds a fiery kick to the salad topping. You can make it yourself or find it at a specialty food store. In a pinch, use sambal oelek, an Indonesian hot pepper sauce that you can pick up at many supermarkets. If serving this to vegans, simply omit the cheese. Cinsault, a Rhône Valley wine varietal, accompanies the pancakes well, as it will stand up to the spicy harissa and dandelion greens, bring out the sweetness of the caramelized onion and root vegetables, and enhance the smoky cumin seeds.

Pancake

¾ cup chickpea (garbanzo bean) flour, preferably Bob's Red Mill

½ teaspoon salt

1 cup water

3 tablespoons extra-virgin olive oil

1 large yellow onion, thinly sliced

1 teaspoon cumin seeds, toasted

Aleppo pepper or freshly ground black pepper

Salad

¼ cup extra-virgin olive oil

2 tablespoons fresh lemon juice

1 garlic clove, finely grated or crushed with a garlic press

2 teaspoons to 2 tablespoons harissa, homemade (page 213) or purchased, or sambal oelek

4 cups trimmed dandelion greens or arugula

1 bunch salad (baby) turnips, trimmed and thinly sliced

3 ounces soft fresh goat cheese or feta cheese, crumbled

For the pancake: Combine the flour and salt in a medium bowl. Whisk in the water and 1 tablespoon of the oil until smooth. Cover the batter loosely and let stand at room temperature for 4 to 8 hours.

Heat 1 tablespoon of the remaining oil in a well-seasoned 10-inch (9 inches on the bottom) cast-iron skillet over medium heat. Add the onion and sauté until golden brown and tender, about 8 minutes. Reduce the heat to medium-low and sauté until the onion is well browned and caramelized, about 8 minutes longer.

recipe continues

For the salad: Whisk together the oil, lemon juice, garlic, and harissa to taste to blend in a small bowl or jar and set aside.

To cook the pancake: Preheat the oven to 450°F.

Place the skillet in the oven and heat until very hot, about 15 minutes. Working quickly, pour the remaining 1 tablespoon oil into the skillet and carefully swirl to evenly coat the bottom of the skillet. Whisk the batter and pour it into the skillet. Scatter the caramelized onions over the surface of the batter and sprinkle with the cumin seeds and pepper. Bake until golden brown and set, about 15 minutes.

For finishing: Toss the greens and turnips with the dressing in a medium bowl. Transfer the pancake to a plate, spoon over the salad, sprinkle with cheese, and serve immediately.

CHICKPEA PANCAKES

Chickpea pancakes are enjoyed in many parts of the world for their rustic flavor, velvety texture, and easy nutrition. The versatile dish takes the form of socca in Provence, farinata in Italy and Argentina, and calentita or calentica in Gibraltar and Algeria. In the U.S., the dish is usually called a chickpea pancake, which lacks poetry and can lead to confusion about griddles and syrup, but by any name, this humble "cake" should play a part in your vegetarian meal rotation. Made with just chickpea (aka garbanzo bean) flour, water, oil and a little salt, the protein-rich and satisfying pancake comes together quickly and can be adapted to whatever you have on hand. Sautéed onions and peppers, pitted olives, grated cheese, chopped herbs, and toasted spices can be added to the pancake before cooking. Once baked, the pancakes can be topped with mixed greens and shaved fresh or sautéed vegetables. It even comes in handy on pizza night as a gluten-free "crust" for wheat-free friends.

toppings, sauces, spreads

harissa

MAKES ABOUT 2 CUPS

Harissa comes in many variations: a fiery-hot drizzle, a carrot-and-caraway-enhanced paste, an oily salsa. My favorite uses sweet, musty guajillo chiles and a dash of coriander and caraway. I keep a jar of it in my refrigerator because it's a way to boost the flavor of sandwiches, grain bowls, and eggs on toast, among other things. Look for both the guajillo chiles and the spices at your local Latin market.

4½ ounces dried guajillo chiles

2 cups water

3 tablespoons extra-virgin olive oil, plus more for drizzling

1 rounded tablespoon coriander seeds

1 rounded teaspoon caraway seeds

½ teaspoon salt

Remove the stems and seeds from the chiles and tear the chiles into 1- to 2-inch pieces.

Have the water ready by the stove. Heat the oil in a heavy large pot over medium-high heat. Add the coriander and caraway seeds and stir briefly until just fragrant, about 30 seconds. Add the chiles and stir until coated with oil and spices but not browned, about 30 seconds. Pour in the water, cover, and cook, stirring occasionally, until the water evaporates, about 8 minutes. Mix in the salt and cool.

Transfer the mixture to a food processor and process into a thick paste. Spoon the harissa into a jar and smooth the top. Pour a small amount of oil into the jar just to cover the surface of the harissa. Seal the jar tightly. *(The harissa can be prepared up to 2 weeks ahead. Keep refrigerated.)*

piri-piri sauce

MAKES ABOUT ¾ CUP

If you like hot sauce very hot, you can make piri-piri with bird's-eye chiles, the small fiery ones often marked as Thai red chiles. Personally, I want to taste the bay, cilantro, and lemon zest, so I prefer to make piri-piri with a medium-hot chile.

4 ounces medium-hot red chiles, such as Korean long peppers, Fresno chiles, or red jalapeño chiles

¼ cup extra-virgin olive oil

¼ cup red wine vinegar

1 tablespoon fresh cilantro leaves

2 (½ x 2-inch) strips lemon zest

1 large garlic clove, peeled

1 fresh bay leaf

½ teaspoon smoked or sweet paprika

½ teaspoon salt

Trim the stems and seeds from the chiles and cut the chiles into ½-inch pieces. (You should have about ¾ cup.) Combine the chiles, oil, vinegar, cilantro, lemon zest, garlic, bay leaf, paprika, and salt in a blender and blend, stopping the blender to scrape the sides down once or twice, until smooth. *(The sauce can be prepared up to 2 weeks ahead. Transfer to a jar and keep refrigerated.)*

zhoug

MAKES ABOUT 1 CUP

Zhoug is a fragrant, green hot sauce from Yemen. The combination of herbs, chiles, and spice makes for an enticing and popular condiment. I like to have a batch in my refrigerator at all times because of its transformative powers—just a spoonful in yogurt, on rice or steamed vegetables, or spread on a sandwich adds the best oomph, and stored with a thin layer of olive oil on top, it lasts a very long time.

1 cup coarsely chopped fresh cilantro leaves and stems (about 1 bunch)

2 large jalapeño chiles, sliced

½ cup coarsely chopped fresh Italian parsley

1 green onion, sliced (about ¼ cup)

2 large garlic cloves, peeled

½ teaspoon cumin seeds

½ teaspoon cardamom seeds (removed from their pods), lightly crushed

½ teaspoon salt

½ teaspoon Aleppo pepper

½ cup extra-virgin olive oil, plus more for drizzling

Combine the cilantro, chiles, parsley, green onion, garlic, cumin, cardamom, salt, and Aleppo pepper in a food processor. Pulse using on/off turns until the mixture is finely chopped, scraping down the edges as needed. Add the oil and process until a coarse puree forms. Transfer the mixture to a jar. Pour a thin layer of oil atop the sauce, if necessary, to cover the herbs and spices completely. Seal the jar and refrigerate for up to 2 weeks. *(Be sure to store unused zhoug with a thin layer of olive oil on the surface to keep it from spoiling.)*

cashew cream

MAKES ABOUT 2 CUPS

This easy-to-make cashew cream can be used in place of goat cheese, burrata, and ricotta. When thinned with the soaking liquid, it can be used in place of sour cream, labneh, or yogurt. Hints of lemon and herbs give the creamy blend the flavor of fresh goat cheese, but you can customize the cashew cream to your taste by adding fresh chives, cracked pepper, roasted garlic, fresh dill, or green garlic. If you don't plan on eating the cashew cream all at once, it will keep in the refrigerator, or you can divide the cream and freeze half for later use.

2 cups raw cashews

2 tablespoons extra-virgin olive oil

1 garlic clove, peeled

½ teaspoon grated lemon zest

2 teaspoons fresh lemon juice

½ teaspoon fresh thyme leaves

¼ teaspoon fresh rosemary leaves

1 teaspoon salt, or more to taste

Combine the cashews and enough water to cover by 3 inches in a medium bowl and soak overnight.

Drain the cashews, reserving ½ cup of the soaking liquid. Combine the cashews, oil, garlic, lemon zest, lemon juice, salt, thyme, rosemary, and salt in a food processor. Process until a puree forms, adding the reserved soaking liquid by the tablespoon as necessary to form a thick, smooth puree. Season with additional salt to taste. Transfer the cream to a food storage container and store in the refrigerator for up to 1 week.

salsa macha

MAKES 2 CUPS

Salsa macha is a fiery sauce of chiles blended with oil, peanuts, and/or sesame seeds. I first tasted salsa macha while in Guanajuato and was instantly smitten. I bought a jar and drizzled it on everything for a piquant kick. Salsa macha is made with various kinds of dried chiles, but I like the subtle smoky flavor that dried chipotle chiles give the sauce. Look for dried chipotles at Mexican markets, specialty foods stores, or online. If you like your salsa fiery, you can double the arbol chiles. I give the option of using olive oil or peanut oil in the recipe, but you can blend the oils to your taste.

2 ounces dried chipotle chiles, stemmed and seeds shaken out (about 1⅓ cups)

1½ cups extra-virgin olive or peanut oil

4 dried arbol chiles, stemmed and seeds shaken out

½ cup shelled peanuts

¼ cup (1¼ ounces) raw sesame seeds

5 garlic cloves, peeled

2 tablespoons apple cider vinegar

1 tablespoon brown sugar

1 teaspoon salt

Tear or cut the chipotles with scissors into 1-inch pieces. Heat 1 cup of the oil in a large cast-iron skillet over medium heat. Add the chipotle and arbol chiles, the peanuts, sesame seeds, and garlic and stir until the chiles are fragrant and soften slightly and the garlic and sesame seeds turn golden, about 3 minutes. Transfer the mixture to a blender and cool slightly. Add the remaining ½ cup oil, the vinegar, brown sugar, and salt and puree. Transfer the salsa to a jar. *(The salsa macha can be stored in the refrigerator for up to 2 months. Allow to come to room temperature and stir well before using.)*

tamarind chutney sauce

MAKES ABOUT ⅓ CUP

If you have ever eaten at an Indian buffet, you're likely familiar with this sweet-tart dark brown dipping sauce. In addition to the Red Quinoa and Red Kidney Bean Masala (page 126) salad, it's delicious on samosas and pakoras.

3 tablespoons brown sugar

2 tablespoons water

1 tablespoon tamarind puree

½ teaspoon garam masala

½ teaspoon ground ginger

¼ teaspoon ground red chile, such as Guntur or cayenne

¼ teaspoon salt

Stir together the ingredients to blend in a small bowl or jar. *(The tamarind chutney can be prepared ahead. Cover and refrigerate for up to 2 weeks.)*

garlicky yogurt

MAKES 1 GENEROUS CUP

I use European-style whole-milk yogurt for this recipe, but if strained or Greek yogurt is what you have, you can thin the mixture with a little milk or kefir if you want a drizzling consistency.

1 cup plain whole-milk yogurt, Greek or regular

1 tablespoon extra-virgin olive oil

1 scant teaspoon salt

2 garlic cloves, finely grated or crushed with a garlic press

Stir together the ingredients to blend in a medium bowl. *(The yogurt can be prepared up to 4 days ahead; cover and refrigerate.)*

pesto drizzle

MAKES ABOUT 2 CUPS

In summer when basil is plentiful, I always have a jar of pesto on hand. I like to mix it with additional olive oil so that I can drizzle salads, pasta, pizza, sandwiches, and platters of grilled vegetables with a burst of bright green flavor.

2 cups fresh basil leaves	3 garlic cloves, peeled
½ cup freshly grated Parmesan cheese	About ½ cup extra-virgin olive oil
½ cup pine nuts, lightly toasted	Salt

Combine the basil, cheese, pine nuts, and garlic in the bowl of the food processor. Gradually add half of the oil and process until smooth. Add enough additional oil to thin to drizzling consistency. Season with salt. *(The pesto drizzle can be made up to 1 week ahead. Transfer to a jar, seal, and refrigerate.)*

romesco sauce

MAKES ABOUT 1⅓ CUPS

Every book I have written includes a recipe for this heady Spanish condiment. I've made it so many ways: with fresh roasted red peppers, peppers from a jar, jarred piquillo peppers, blended with almonds or hazelnuts—any way, it's delicious. Try it with roasted potatoes, grilled zucchini, thickly spread on sandwiches, or with poached eggs and salad greens.

2 large red bell peppers, or 1 generous cup jarred roasted peppers (one 12-ounce jar)	3 garlic cloves, peeled
⅓ cup almonds, toasted	1 tablespoon hot or sweet smoked paprika
¼ cup extra-virgin olive oil	1 tablespoon sherry vinegar
	Salt

If using fresh peppers, char them over a gas flame on the stovetop or under the broiler until blackened and charred on all sides. Transfer to a bowl and cover with plastic wrap. Allow the peppers to steam as they cool. Peel, seed, and slice the peppers.

Combine the roasted or jarred peppers, almonds, oil, garlic, smoked paprika, and vinegar in a blender and blend until smooth. Season with salt. *(The romesco can be prepared up to 1 week ahead. Transfer to a jar and refrigerate.)*

spicy coconut peanut sauce

MAKES ABOUT 2½ CUPS

My kids used to play a game: think of
a food that doesn't taste good with
peanuts or peanut butter. It's tough, and
this slightly sweet and spicy sauce is super
on most savory foods, especially my
versions of gado-gado. Made quickly with
pantry staples, the sauce is a delicious
way to bring flavor and focus to random
foods in the cupboard and crisper. I find
myself whisking up a batch to spoon over
brown rice and shredded cabbage for a
quick lunch, enjoy as a dip for cucumbers
and carrots, drizzle over grilled tofu, or
toss with leftover cooked vegetables.

¾ cup natural
peanut butter

¾ cup (or more)
unsweetened
canned coconut
milk

⅓ cup rice vinegar

⅓ cup soy sauce or
tamari

¼ cup brown sugar

3 tablespoons
sambal oelek or
sriracha

3 garlic cloves,
finely grated or
pressed with a
garlic press

Whisk together all the ingredients to
blend in a medium bowl. *(The sauce can
be made up to 1 week ahead; cover and
keep refrigerated.)*

preserved lemons

MAKES TWO 8-OUNCE JARS

Cooks in North Africa began preserving
lemons in salt around the tenth century.
Putting lemons up in salt meant that
their tart, bright flavor could be enjoyed
in dishes when fresh lemons were not in
season. Salty and sour, preserved lemons
have a unique and enticing flavor—a jar or
two should always be in your refrigerator.
After removing the desired amount of
preserved lemons from the jar, be sure
that the remaining lemons are completely
covered with olive oil—you may need to
add a touch more.

3 or 4 lemons,
preferably Meyer
lemons

About ¼ cup
Diamond Crystal
kosher salt

Extra-virgin olive
oil

Wash and dry the lemons and cut
lengthwise into quarters. Place 1 lemon
quarter into each of two 8-ounce jars.
Sprinkle the lemon generously with salt.
Repeat, nestling enough lemon quarters
into each jar to fill it completely, pressing
gently on the lemons and sprinkling with
salt after each addition. Pour enough
oil into the jars to cover the lemons by
½ inch. Seal the jars and refrigerate for
at least 1 week before using. *(The lemons
can be made several months ahead. Keep
the lemons refrigerated, making sure they
are completely submerged in lemon juice
and olive oil. To use, chop the peel and pulp
of the preserved lemon and discard the
seeds.)*

ancho-spiced pecans

MAKES 2 CUPS

These mildly spiced sweet-and-salty nuts add fun crunch to salads but also make a crave-worthy nibble to enjoy by the handful or with cocktails.

¼ cup brown sugar

1 tablespoon water

1½ teaspoons ancho chile powder

1 scant teaspoon salt

Pinch of ground cloves

2 cups pecan halves

Preheat the oven to 325°F. Line a heavy large sheet pan with a silicone baking mat or parchment paper.

In a large bowl, stir together the brown sugar, water, chile powder, salt, and cloves to blend. Add the pecans and toss to coat thoroughly. Spread the pecans out in a single layer on the prepared sheet pan. Roast until lightly browned and glazed, about 20 minutes. Cool completely, transfer to a jar, and cover. *(The pecans can be made up to 1 week ahead. Store at room temperature.)*

rustic croutons

MAKES ABOUT 2 CUPS

A fresh loaf of rustic sourdough, whether home-baked or picked up at an artisanal bakery, stays fresh for only so long. I often find myself baking or buying a fresh boule while a quarter loaf sits a little dry and forlorn on my breadboard. Never wanting to waste a good crumb, I cut the less-than-fresh ends of bread into cubes and store them in bags in the freezer. Thawed and toasted with olive oil, they can transform a salad into a solid meal.

3 tablespoons extra-virgin olive oil

1 garlic clove, finely grated or crushed with a garlic press

2 cups ½-inch rustic bread cubes

Salt

Preheat the oven to 400°F.

Stir the oil and garlic in a medium bowl to blend. Add the bread cubes and toss to coat with the oil mixture. Transfer the bread cubes to a heavy sheet pan, sprinkle with salt and toast until golden brown, stirring once, about 8 minutes. Cool. *(The croutons can be made up to 6 hours ahead. Cover and store at room temperature.)*

acknowledgments

Big thanks!

When spending days at the kitchen counter and in front of a laptop, the process of writing a cookbook can feel overwhelmingly solitary. But in truth, there's an entire team of people that help with the production and creative process. I make special effort to give credit to the cooks who have directly influenced salads in this book by name, but there are also the way-too-many-to list cookbook authors, chefs, food writers, food bloggers, radio hosts, editors, home cooks, farmers, gardeners, friends, neighbors, and even strangers who have knowingly (and unknowingly!) taught and inspired me over the years—there's a little bit of you on these pages.

Special appreciation to Gemma and Andrew Ingalls for the beautiful photography and help with artistic vision. Our shoots were always cheery, and I feel extra lucky that you were always willing to share so many of your own special platters, bowls, linens, and flatware for our "salad-scapes." Unlike most cookbooks, where photography takes place in a studio or rented home with a team of food and prop stylists, the salads you see on these pages were assembled by me in my home kitchen. Our shoots took place throughout the year in order to capture seasonal produce at its peak. (Thank you again, Gemma and Andy!) Niki Ford, Natatcha Stojanovic, and Isabel Hees lent their talent, energy, and excellent cooking assistance to shoot days, and I am forever grateful for their creativity and camaraderie.

I've used a variety of lovely ceramic pieces in this book, including hand-crafted pieces by Gopi Shah, Coco Chispa, and the People's Pottery Project, but special thanks go to Mt. Washington Pottery for lending me a box full of their beautiful bowls, plates, and pourers.

Special mention goes to my agent, Deborah Ritchken; editor, Martynka Wawrzyniak; book designer, Jan Derevjanik; Ivy McFadden; Leda Sheintaub; and the folks at Rizzoli for all their help in nurturing, guiding, and composing this beautiful book.

Lastly—my gratitude and love go to my very large and expanding salad-loving family; to my daughters, Celeste and Theresa, who are honest critics with exceptional taste; to my sons-in-law, Dylan and Dillon, who will eat anything I serve them; and especially to my husband, Martin, whose patience, kindness, and ability to grow the best salad greens ever have no bounds.

VEGETARIAN SALAD FOR DINNER

index

acorn squash. *see winter squash*
Ancho-Spiced Pecans, 219
Artichoke with Sambuca, Pasta, Ricotta Salata, 152, *153*
arugula, about, 13
   Arugula Cacio e Pepe Pizza, 167
   Carrot, Bulgur, Green Olives, Arugula, Date, Preserved Lemon, *8*, 58, *59*
   Fregola, Fennel, Olive, Pecorino, Orange, Arugula, *150*, 151
   Quinoa, Spring Vegetables, Arugula, Kumquats, Pistachios, *17*, 116, 117
   Roasted Asparagus, Broccolini, Feta, Meyer Lemon, Green Garlic, Arugula, Pistachio Dukkah, 200, *201*
   Roasted Delicata, Goat Cheese, Arugula, Almond Charmoul, *198*, 199
asparagus
   Breaded Baked Goat Cheese, Frisée, Wild Mushrooms, Asparagus, 169, *171*
   Fava Beans, Asparagus, Toasted Couscous, Spring Herbs, Preserved Lemon, Labneh, *154*, 155
   Roasted Asparagus, Broccolini, Feta, Meyer Lemon, Green Garlic, Arugula, Pistachio Dukkah, 200, *201*
avocado, about, 44
   Baby Gem, Hearts of Palm, Avocado, Radish, Marcona Almonds, Green Goddess, 46, *47*
   Coconut Quinoa, Black Beans, Avocado, Mango, Collards, Plantain, Cashews, *128*, 129
   Creamy Lime-Avocado Dressing, 44
   Kohlrabi, Avocado, Egg, Radicchio, Watercress, Mustard-Poppy Vinaigrette, 134, *135*

barley
   Mushrooms, Barley, Dandelion Greens, 80
   Sweet Sesame Barley, Kale, Tofu, *2*, 62, *63*
bean salads. *see beans; chickpeas; lentils*
beans, dried/canned. *see also black beans; mung beans*
   Corona Bean Salad, 88, *89*
   Grilled Broccoli, Mushrooms, Peppers, White Bean Puree, Chimichurri, 110, *111*
   Red Quinoa and Red Kidney Bean Masala, 126, *127*
   White Bean, Broiled Treviso, Fig, Olive, 106, *107*
beans, green. *see also fava beans; long*

beans; romano beans
   Charred Green Beans and Parsnips, Farro, Radicchio, Gorgonzola, Walnuts, 82, 83
   Corona Bean Salad, 88, *89*
beets
   Beet Hummus, Fioretto, Pine Nut Gremolata, 97, *99*
   Beet, Buckwheat, Walnuts, Greens, Goat Gouda, *132*, 133
   French Lentils, Roasted Beets, Dried Cherries, Rosemary, Goat Cheese, 90, *91*
   Roasted Beets, Citrus, Labneh, Zhoug, 204, *205*
Belgian endive, about, 13
black beans
   Black Beans, Brown Rice, Scorched Kale, *104*, 105
   Coconut Quinoa, Black Beans, Avocado, Mango, Collards, Plantain, Cashews, *128*, 129
   Tostada Salad, Creamy Lime-Avocado Dressing, 43, *45*
   Black Garlic Tofu, Black Rice, Snap Peas, Pea Sprouts, 67, *69*
black lentils. *see lentils*
black quinoa. *see quinoa*
black rice, about, 68
   Black Rice, Snap Peas, Pea Sprouts, Black Garlic Tofu, 67, *69*
bread salads
   Breaded Baked Goat Cheese, Frisée, Wild Mushrooms, Asparagus, 169, *171*
   Broccoli Salad with Olive, Pecorino, Lemon, Croutons, 179
   Chopped Salad, Migas, Spanish Goodies, *4*, 175, *177*
   Fall Bread Salad, *182*, 183
   Herby Fattoush, Sumac-Cumin Pita Crisps, *9*, *172*, 173
   Spring Panzanella, Creamy Pecorino Dressing, *12*, 184, *185*
   Summer Panzanella, Burrata, Pesto Drizzle, 180, *181*
broccoli
   Broccoli Salad with Olive, Pecorino, Lemon, Croutons, 179
   Grilled Broccoli, Mushrooms, Peppers, White Bean Puree, Chimichurri, 110, *111*
   Roasted Broccoli, Preserved Lemon, Calabrian Chile, Whole Wheat Pasta, *157*, 158
   Broccolini, Roasted Asparagus, Feta, Meyer Lemon, Green Garlic, Arugula, Pistachio Dukkah, 200, *201*
Brussels sprouts
   Brussels Sprouts, Wild Rice, Ancho-Spiced Pecans, Dates, Goat Cheese, 76, *77*

   Warm Brussels Sprout Caesar, Poached Egg, *26*, 27
buckwheat
   Beet, Buckwheat, Walnuts, Greens, Goat Gouda, *132*, 133
   Buckwheat Soba, Kabocha Squash, Walnuts, Persimmon, Greens, *144*, 145
   Grilled Sweet Potatoes, Kale, Garlicky Yogurt, Puffed Buckwheat, *124*, 125
bulgur
   Carrot, Bulgur, Green Olives, Arugula, Date, Preserved Lemon, *8*, 58, *59*
   Grape (or Plum), Fennel, Tabbouleh, Goat Cheese "Cream," Saba, *60*, 61
   Burrata, Summer Panzanella, Pesto Drizzle, 180, *181*
butternut squash.
      see winter squash

cabbage, about, 14
   Acorn Squash, Wilted Red Cabbage, Apple, Pumpkin Seed Dressing, 121, *123*
   Black Lentil, Roast Cauliflower, Red Cabbage Slaw, Piri-Piri Sauce, 102, *103*
Caponata, Eggplant, Ricotta Salata, Celery Leaves, 34, *35*
carrots
   Carrot, Bulgur, Green Olives, Arugula, Date, Preserved Lemon, *8*, 58, *59*
   Roasted Spiced Carrots, Quinoa, Chickpeas, Green Ribbons, Turmeric Vinaigrette, *118*, 119
Cashew Cream, 214
cauliflower
   Black Lentil, Roast Cauliflower, Red Cabbage Slaw, Piri-Piri Sauce, 102, *103*
   Chickpeas, Cauliflower, Tomato, Sumac Yogurt, *8–9*, 188, *189*
   Lettuce Cups, Thai Flavors, Cauliflower, Tempeh, 48, *49*
   Whole Roasted Cauliflower, Mung Beans, Greens, Black Tahını, *190*, 191
Charmoula, Almond, Delicata, Roasted, Goat Cheese, Arugula, *198*, 199
chickpeas/chickpea flour
   chickpea pancakes, about, 210
   Chickpeas, Cauliflower, Tomato, Sumac Yogurt, *8–9*, 188, *189*
   Chopped Salad, Migas, Spanish Goodies, *4*, 175, *177*
   Hummus Msabaha, Curly Endive, Zhoug, 100, 101

chickpeas/chickpea flour (cont.)
North African–Style Chickpea Pancake, Salad Turnips, Greens, Harissa, 208, *209*
Panisse, 42
Roasted Spiced Carrots, Quinoa, Chickpeas, Green Ribbons, Turmeric Vinaigrette, *118, 119*
Chimichurri, Grilled Broccoli, Mushrooms, Peppers, White Bean Puree, 110, *111*
chopped salads
Chopped Salad, Migas, Spanish Goodies, 4, 175, *177*
Italian Chopped Salad, 24, *25*
collard greens, about 14
Coconut Quinoa, Black Beans, Avocado, Mango, Collards, Plantain, Cashews, *128, 129*
Corona Bean Salad, 88, *89*
couscous
Couscous, Saffron Gem, Smashed Cucumbers with Mint, Greens, Pomegranate Vinaigrette, 147, *149*
Fava Beans, Asparagus, Toasted Couscous, Spring Herbs, Preserved Lemon, Labneh, *154, 155*
Croutons, Rustic, 219
Cucumbers, Smashed, with Mint, 148
curly endive, about, 14
Hummus Msabaha, Curly Endive, Zhoug, *100,* 101

dandelion greens, about, 14
Dandelion Greens, Roasted Potatoes, Romesco, 4, 195, *194*
Muhammara, Turnip, Pomegranate, and Dandelion Green Slaw, Walnuts, 8, 92, *93*
Mushrooms, Barley, Dandelion Greens, 80
North African–Style Chickpea Pancake, Salad Turnips, Greens, Harissa, 208, *209*
dates
Brussels Sprouts, Wild Rice, Ancho-Spiced Pecans, Dates, Goat Cheese, 76, *77*
Carrot, Bulgur, Green Olives, Arugula, Date, Preserved Lemon, 8, 58, *59*
Delicata, Roasted, Goat Cheese, Arugula, Almond Charmoul, *198,* 199
dressing, salad. *see salad dressing,*
Dukkah, Pistachio, Roasted Asparagus, Broccolini, Feta, Meyer Lemon, Green Garlic, Arugula, 200, *201*

eggplant
Eggplant Caponata, Ricotta Salata, Celery Leaves, 34, *35*
Falafel-ette Salad, 94, *95*
eggs
Indonesian Gado-Gado Salad, Spicy Peanut Sauce, 38, *39*
Kohlrabi, Avocado, Egg, Radicchio, Watercress, Mustard-Poppy Vinaigrette, 134, *135*
Pink Rice, Long Bean, Lime Leaf,

Fresh Turmeric, Sambal Egg, *64,* 65
Sambal Eggs, 66
Soy Eggs, 30, *31*
Sprouted Grain Toasties, Egg Salad, Ricotta, Herbs, 164, *165*
Warm Brussels Sprout Caesar, Poached Egg, *26,* 27
endive. *see Belgian endive; curly endive,*

Falafel-ette Salad, 94, *95*
farro
Charred Green Beans and Parsnips, Farro, Radicchio, Gorgonzola, Walnuts, *82,* 83
Crispy Farro, Winter Greens, Persimmon, Pomegranate, Hazelnuts, *70,* 71
Summer Succotash Salad, Herb Dressing, *74,* 75
Fattoush, Herby, Sumac-Cumin Pita Crisps, *9, 172, 173*
fava beans
Arroz con Cosas (Paella-Style Salad), 4, 84, *85*
Fava Beans, Asparagus, Toasted Couscous, Spring Herbs, Preserved Lemon, Labneh, *154, 155*
fennel
Fregola, Fennel, Olive, Pecorino, Orange, Arugula, *150,* 151
Grape (or Plum), Fennel, Tabbouleh, Goat Cheese "Cream," Saba, *60,* 61
Italian Chopped Salad, 24, *25*
Quinoa, Spring Vegetables, Arugula, Kumquats, Pistachios, *17, 116, 117*
feta cheese
Black Quinoa, Black Lentils, Pomegranate, Orange, Honey Baked Feta, 130, *131*
Roasted Asparagus, Broccolini, Feta, Meyer Lemon, Green Garlic, Arugula, Pistachio Dukkah, 200, *201*
Fig, White Bean, Broiled Treviso, Olive, 106, *107*
Fioretto, Beet Hummus, Pine Nut Gremolata, 97, *99*
Freekeh Salad, Zucchini and, Za'atar, Halloumi, 72, *73*
Fregola, Fennel, Olive, Pecorino, Orange, Arugula, *150,* 151
frisée, about, 14
Breaded Baked Goat Cheese, Frisée, Wild Mushrooms, Asparagus, 169, *171*

Gado-Gado Salad, Indonesian, Spicy Peanut Sauce, 38, *39*
garlic, black. *see black garlic*
Ginger-Sesame Noodles, Salad, Cashews, 160
goat cheese
Breaded Baked Goat Cheese, Frisée, Wild Mushrooms, Asparagus, 169, *171*
Brussels Sprouts, Wild Rice, Ancho-Spiced Pecans, Dates, Goat Cheese, 76, *77*

French Lentils, Roasted Beets, Dried Cherries, Rosemary, Goat Cheese, 90, *91*
Grape (or Plum), Fennel, Tabbouleh, Goat Cheese "Cream," Saba, *60,* 61
Roasted Delicata, Goat Cheese, Arugula, Almond Charmoul, *198,* 199
Salade Provençal, Panisse, Lemon-Chèvre Dressing, 40, *41*
grain salads. *see barley; buckwheat; bulgur; farro; freekeh; quinoa; rice; wild rice*
Greek Salad, Greek Fava Dip, 53, *55*
green beans. *see beans, green*
Green Goddess Dressing, 47
gremolata, about, 98

Harissa, 213
herbs (as salad greens), about, 15
hummus
Beet Hummus, Fioretto, Pine Nut Gremolata, 97, *99*
Hummus Msabaha, Curly Endive, Zhoug, *100,* 101

Indonesian Gado-Gado Salad, Spicy Peanut Sauce, 38, *39*
Italian Chopped Salad, 24, *25*

kabocha squash. *see winter squash*
kale, about, 15
Black Beans, Brown Rice, Scorched Kale, *104,* 105
Grilled Sweet Potatoes, Kale, Garlicky Yogurt, Puffed Buckwheat, *124,* 125
Roasted Whole Butternut Squash, Salsa Macha, Kale, Cotija Cheese, *196,* 197
Sweet Sesame Barley, Kale, Tofu, 2, *62, 63*
Kohlrabi, Avocado, Egg, Radicchio, Watercress, Mustard-Poppy Vinaigrette, 134, *135*
Kumquats, Quinoa, Spring Vegetables, Arugula, Pistachios, *17, 116, 117*

Lemons, Preserved, 218
lentils
Black Lentil, Roast Cauliflower, Red Cabbage Slaw, Piri-Piri Sauce, 102, *103*
Black Quinoa, Black Lentils, Pomegranate, Orange, Honey Baked Feta, 130, *131*
French Lentils, Roasted Beets, Dried Cherries, Rosemary, Goat Cheese, 90, *91*
lettuce. 14, 15, 16. *see also salad greens*
Lime-Avocado Dressing, Creamy, 44
Long Bean, Pink Rice, Lime Leaf, Fresh Turmeric, Sambal Egg, 64, 65

mangoes
Coconut Quinoa, Black Beans, Avocado, Mango, Collards, Plantain, Cashews, *128,* 129
Potato, Pea, Mango, Yogurt, Spice, Spinach, *108,* 109

Migas, Chopped Salad, Spanish Goodies, 4, 175, *177*

mizuna, about, 15
Buckwheat Soba, Kabocha Squash, Walnuts, Persimmon, Greens, 144, 145
Heirloom Salad, Creamy Sesame-Miso Tofu, *136*, 137
Msabaha, Hummus, Curly Endive, Zhoug, 100, 101
Muhammara, Turnip, Pomegranate, and Dandelion Green Slaw, Walnuts, 8, 92, *93*

mung beans
Mung Beans, Caramelized Onions, Sun-Dried Tomatoes, 112, 113
Whole Roasted Cauliflower, Mung Beans, Greens, Black Tahini, 190, 191

mushrooms
Breaded Baked Goat Cheese, Frisée, Wild Mushrooms, Asparagus, 169, *171*
Grilled Broccoli, Mushrooms, Peppers, White Bean Puree, Chimichurri, 110, *111*
Mushrooms, Barley, Dandelion Greens, 80

oakleaf lettuce, about, 15
Heirloom Salad, Creamy Sesame-Miso Tofu, *136*, 137

olives
Broccoli Salad with Olive, Pecorino, Lemon, Croutons, 179
Carrot, Bulgur, Green Olives, Arugula, Date, Preserved Lemon, 8, 58, *59*
Fregola, Fennel, Olive, Pecorino, Orange, Arugula, *150*, 151
White Bean, Broiled Treviso, Fig, Olive, 106, *107*
Onions, Caramelized, Mung Beans, Sun-Dried Tomatoes, 112, 113

oranges
Black Quinoa, Black Lentils, Pomegranate, Orange, Honey Baked Feta, 130, *131*
Fregola, Fennel, Olive, Pecorino, Orange, Arugula, *150*, 151
Orecchiette, Tomato-Herb Salsa Cruda, 156, *157*
Orzo, Loaded, *157*, 159

Paella-Style Salad (Arroz con Cosas), 4, 84, 85
Panisse, 42

panzanella
Spring Panzanella, Creamy Pecorino Dressing, *12*, 184, *185*
Summer Panzanella, Burrata, Pesto Drizzle, 180, *181*
Parsnips, Charred Green Beans and, Farro, Radicchio, Gorgonzola, Walnuts, *82*, 83

pasta salads
Artichoke with Sambuca, Pasta, Ricotta Salata, 152, *153*
Buckwheat Soba, Kabocha Squash, Walnuts, Persimmon, Greens, *144*, 145

Fava Beans, Asparagus, Toasted Couscous, Spring Herbs, Preserved Lemon, Labneh, *154*, 155
Fregola, Fennel, Olive, Pecorino, Orange, Arugula, *150*, 151
Ginger-Sesame Noodles, Salad, Cashews, 160
Loaded Orzo, *157*, 159
Orecchiette, Tomato-Herb Salsa Cruda, 156, *157*
Pesto Zoodles and Noodles, 142, *143*
Roasted Broccoli, Preserved Lemon, Calabrian Chile, Whole Wheat Pasta, *157*, 158
Saffron Gem Couscous, Smashed Cucumbers with Mint, Greens, Pomegranate Vinaigrette, 147, *149*
Pea Sprouts, Black Rice, Snap Peas, Black Garlic Tofu, 67, *69*
Pecans, Ancho-Spiced, 219

pepitas. *see pumpkin seeds*

peppers, bell. *see also roasted peppers*
Baked Ricotta Pepperonata, Herb Salad, *206*, 207
Grilled Broccoli, Mushrooms, Peppers, White Bean Puree, Chimichurri, 110, *111*
Romesco Sauce, 216

persimmons
Buckwheat Soba, Kabocha Squash, Walnuts, Persimmon, Greens, *144*, 145
Crispy Farro, Winter Greens, Persimmon, Pomegranate, Hazelnuts, *70*, 71

pesto
Pesto Drizzle, 216
Pesto Zoodles and Noodles, 142, *143*
Piri-Piri Sauce, 213
Pita Crisps, Sumac-Cumin, 174
Pizza, Cacio e Pepe, Arugula, 167
Plantain, Coconut Quinoa, Black Beans, Avocado, Mango, Collards, Cashews, *128*, 129

pomegranate molasses, about, 148
Black Quinoa, Black Lentils, Pomegranate, Orange, Honey Baked Feta, 130, *131*
Muhammara, Turnip, Pomegranate, and Dandelion Green Slaw, Walnuts, 8, 92, *93*
Saffron Gem Couscous, Smashed Cucumbers with Mint, Greens, Pomegranate Vinaigrette, 147, *149*

pomegranates
Crispy Farro, Winter Greens, Persimmon, Pomegranate, Hazelnuts, *70*, 71
Muhammara, Turnip, Pomegranate, and Dandelion Green Slaw, Walnuts, 8, 92, *93*

potatoes
Dandelion Greens, Roasted Potatoes, Romesco, 4, 195, *194*
Indonesian Gado-Gado Salad, Spicy Peanut Sauce, 38, *39*
Potato Salad, Lettuce Cups, Herb Gribiche, *32*, 33

Potato, Pea, Mango, Yogurt, Spice, Spinach, *108*, 109
Salade "Gratinée," Roasted Fingerlings, Red Onions, 192, *193*

preserved lemons
Carrot, Bulgur, Green Olives, Arugula, Date, Preserved Lemon, 8, 58, *59*
Fava Beans, Asparagus, Toasted Couscous, Spring Herbs, Preserved Lemon, Labneh, *154*, 155
Preserved Lemons, 218
Roasted Broccoli, Preserved Lemon, Calabrian Chile, Whole Wheat Pasta, *157*, 158
Pumpkin Seed Dressing, Acorn Squash, Wilted Red Cabbage, Apple, 121, *123*

quinoa, about (rinsing), 120
Black Quinoa, Black Lentils, Pomegranate, Orange, Honey Baked Feta, 130, *131*
Coconut Quinoa, Black Beans, Avocado, Mango, Collards, Plantain, Cashews, *128*, 129
Quinoa, Spring Vegetables, Arugula, Kumquats, Pistachios, *17*, 116, 117
Red Quinoa and Red Kidney Bean Masala, 126, *127*
Roasted Spiced Carrots, Quinoa, Chickpeas, Green Ribbons, Turmeric Vinaigrette, 118, 119

radicchio, about, 16
Charred Green Beans and Parsnips, Farro, Radicchio, Gorgonzola, Walnuts, *82*, 83
Kohlrabi, Avocado, Egg, Radicchio, Watercress, Mustard-Poppy Vinaigrette, 134, *135*

rice. *see also wild rice*
Arroz con Cosas (Paella-Style Salad), 4, 84, 85
Black Beans, Brown Rice, Scorched Kale, *104*, 105
black rice, about, 68
Black Rice, Snap Peas, Pea Sprouts, Black Garlic Tofu, 67, *69*
Brown Rice, Grape Leaf Salad, *78*, 79
Korean Bibimbap-Style Salad, Soy Egg, 29, *31*
Pink Rice, Long Bean, Lime Leaf, Fresh Turmeric, Sambal Egg, 64, 65

ricotta
Baked Ricotta Pepperonata, Herb Salad, *206*, 207
Sprouted Grain Toasties, Egg Salad, Ricotta, Herbs, 164, *165*

ricotta salata
Artichoke with Sambuca, Pasta, Ricotta Salata, 152, *153*
Eggplant Caponata, Ricotta Salata, Celery Leaves, 34, *35*

roasted peppers
Muhammara, Turnip, Pomegranate, and Dandelion Green Slaw, Walnuts, 8, 92, *93*

romano beans
Arroz con Cosas (Paella-Style Salad), 4, 84, *85*
Romesco Sauce, 216

salad dressing
Creamy Lime-Avocado Dressing, 44
Free-Free Dressing, 133
Green Goddess Dressing, 47
Lemony Dressing, 174
Oregano Vinaigrette, 54
salad greens, about, 13–16. *see also individual greens*
Salad Rolls, Vietnamese-Style, Hoisin Peanut Sauce, *50*, 51
Salade "Gratinée," Roasted Fingerlings, Red Onions, 192, *193*
Salade Provençal, Panisse, Lemon-Chèvre Dressing, *40*, 41
Salanova lettuce, about, 14
Sambal Eggs, 66
Sambuca, Artichoke with, Pasta, Ricotta Salata, 152, *153*
salt, 21
sauces, savory
Harissa, 213
Hoisin Peanut Sauce, 52
Pesto Drizzle, 216
Piri-Piri Sauce, 213
Romesco Sauce, 216
Salsa Macha, 215
Spicy Coconut Peanut Sauce, 218
Tahini Sauce, 96
Tamarind Chutney Sauce, 215
Zhoug, 214
slaw
Black Lentil, Roast Cauliflower, Red Cabbage Slaw, Piri-Piri Sauce, 102, *103*
Muhammara, Turnip, Pomegranate, and Dandelion Green Slaw, Walnuts, *8*, 92, *93*
Snap Peas, Black Rice, Pea Sprouts, Black Garlic Tofu, 67, *69*
Soba, Buckwheat, Kabocha Squash, Walnuts, Persimmon, Greens, *144*, 145
spinach, about, 16
Potato, Pea, Mango, Yogurt, Spice, Spinach, *108*, 109
Tempeh, Spinach, Peanutty-Lime Dressing, *202*, 203
squash, winter. *see winter squash*,
Succotash Salad, Summer, Herb Dressing, *74*, 75
sumac
Chickpeas, Cauliflower, Tomato, Sumac Yogurt, *8–9*, 188, *189*
Lemony Dressing, 174
Sumac-Cumin Pita Crisps, 174
Sweet Potatoes, Grilled, Kale, Garlicky Yogurt, Puffed Buckwheat, *124*, 125
Swiss chard, about, 16
Tabbouleh, Grape (or Plum), Fennel, Goat Cheese "Cream," Saba, *60*, 61

tahini
Black Tahini, Whole Roasted Cauliflower, Mung Beans, Greens, *190*, 191

Lemony Dressing, 174
Tahini Sauce, 96
Tamarind Chutney Sauce, 215
tatsoi, about, 16
Buckwheat Soba, Kabocha Squash, Walnuts, Persimmon, Greens, *144*, 145
Heirloom Salad, Creamy Sesame-Miso Tofu, *136*, 137
tempeh
Lettuce Cups, Thai Flavors, Cauliflower, Tempeh, 48, *49*
Tempeh, Spinach, Peanutty-Lime Dressing, *202*, 203
tofu
Black Rice, Snap Peas, Pea Sprouts, Black Garlic Tofu, 67, *69*
Heirloom Salad, Creamy Sesame-Miso Tofu, *136*, 137
Sweet Sesame Barley, Kale, Tofu, *2*, 62, *63*
tomatoes
Chickpeas, Cauliflower, Tomato, Sumac Yogurt, *8–9*, 188, *189*
Orecchiette, Tomato-Herb Salsa Cruda, 156, *157*
Treviso, about, 16
White Bean, Broiled Treviso, Fig, Olive, 106, *107*
turnips
Muhammara, Turnip, Pomegranate, and Dandelion Green Slaw, Walnuts, *8*, 92, *93*
North African–Style Chickpea Pancake, Salad Turnips, Greens, Harissa, 208, *209*

Vietnamese-Style Salad Rolls, Hoisin Peanut Sauce, *50*, 51
Vinaigrette, Oregano, 54

watercress, about, 16
Kohlrabi, Avocado, Egg, Radicchio, Watercress, Mustard-Poppy Vinaigrette, 134, *135*
Wild Rice, Brussels Sprouts, Ancho-Spiced Pecans, Dates, Goat Cheese, 76, *77*
winter squash, roasted, about, 122
Acorn Squash, Wilted Red Cabbage, Apple, Pumpkin Seed Dressing, 121, *123*
Buckwheat Soba, Kabocha Squash, Walnuts, Persimmon, Greens, *144*, 145
Roasted Whole Butternut Squash, Salsa Macha, Kale, Cotija Cheese, 196, *197*
Sherry-Simmered Kabocha Squash, 146

Za'atar, Zucchini and Freekeh Salad with Halloumi, 72, *73*
Zhoug, 214
zucchini
Pesto Zoodles and Noodles, 142, *143*
Summer Succotash Salad, Herb Dressing, *74*, 75
Zucchini and Freekeh Salad, Za'atar, Halloumi, 72, *73*

First published in the United States of America in 2023 by Rizzoli International Publications, Inc.
300 Park Avenue South
New York, NY 10010
www.rizzoliusa.com

Copyright © 2023 Jeanne Kelley

Publisher: Charles Miers
Author: Jeanne Kelley
Editor: Martynka Wawrzyniak
Production Manager: Kaija Markoe
Managing Editor: Lynn Scrabis

Photography: The Ingalls
Designer: Jan Derevjanik
Food Stylist: Jeanne Kelley

2023 2024 2025 2026/
10 9 8 7 6 5 4 3 2 1

Printed in China

ISBN: 9780847899401

Library of Congress Control Number: 9780847899401